New & Used
Blab!

New & Used Blab!

EDITED & DESIGNED BY MONTE BEAUCHAMP

CHRONICLE BOOKS • SAN FRANCISCO

Thank you: Jim Heimann, for bringing this project to the attention of Chronicle Books. A very special thanks to: Alan Rapp, for his editorial guidance, good taste, and great ideas; Leslie Davisson, for editorial assistance; Sara Schneider, for design support and coordination; and Steve Kim, for production coordination. With deep gratitude, thank you: Doug Allen, Mark Alvarado, Gary Baseman, Stephane Blanquet, Laurent Bouhnik, Irwin Chusid, Greg Clarke, The Clayton Brothers, Sue Coe, Douglas Fraser, Charles Freund, Drew Friedman, Camille Rose Garcia, David Goldin, Gary Groth, Matti Hagelberg, Becky Hall, Doug Hawk, Jukka Heiskanen, Peter and Maria Hoey, Jem and Scout, Haley Johnson, Peter Kuper, Mark Landman, Walter Minus, Mark Mothersbaugh, Teresa Mucha, Christian Northeast, Eric Reynolds, Jonathon Rosen, Marc Rosenthal, Mark Ryden, Richard Sala, Spain, Jeffrey Steele, Fred Stonehouse, and Kim Thompson.

Designed, Edited, and Produced by: Monte Beauchamp

10 9 8 7 6 5 4 3 2 1

Chronicle Books LLC, 85 Second Street, San Francisco, California 94105. www.chroniclebooks.com

CONTENTS

There's a joke that my grandpa once told me right before he died: "Danny Bonaduce and David Cassidy are up on a hill and there's a bunch of cheerleaders grazing in the grass next to a big red barn. Danny runs over to David laying under a shady tree and cheerfully chirps, 'David, David, let's run down the hill and read a *BLAB!*' David looks him in the eye, yawns and stretches, and then replies, 'Let's walk down the hill, and read 'em all!' " I never fully understood this joke until a journey to Chicago to perform a fake marriage ceremony for some young artists friends led me to a late-night bookstore where I picked up a couple early issues of *BLAB!* and read them on the flight home, skipping the Tom Hanks thing that played on the little screen.

In nightclubs in Africa, the patrons join the local talent at the end of the evening and sing, "There's a reason that I'm itching, so stop your petty bitching, about lions, tanks, dictators, and the like. Any Watusi worth his wiglets, could tell about the piglets, who sit around and read their *BLAB!*s each night. If a missionary chicken, had the pluck for finger-licking, then I'm sure it'd lick its fingers with delight, as it turned each BLABBERIFIC page, of the mag we all are needing, due to chemicals and breeding, let me tell you friend, this *BLAB!* is really the rage!"

If I was going to have to crawl down a dank, dark, dirty, dangerous hell-hole into a nest infested with raging, gnarly, half-crazed terrorists, knowing maybe there was no coming back, I would want to take two things with me: a flame-thrower, and a copy of *BLAB!*—not *Blob!*, *Blub!*, or *Blerb!*, but *BLAB!*

—*Mark Mothersbaugh, Los Angeles*

HORACE

Horace Alden Thayer (1915-1963) was born the only child of Bernard Minsley Thayer, Brooklyn's infamous sausage-casing tycoon. Throughout his youth, Horace was exposed to many privileges but found solace in only one thing—insects. He avidly collected books about them and spent his days foraging his family's vast forested estate in search of entomological treasures.

Fig. 6

The NEW WIENER JUNIOR
featuring THAYER's intestinal casings
to SERVE the whole family

THAYER'S
The best place to stuff your sausage
TRADE MARK

INVOICE
Thayer's Intestinal Casings, Inc.
makers of sausage casings

SOLD TO

Horace Alden Thayer
Place of birth Feb. 22 1915
Date of birth   hair Brown   7
eyes Blue   Ht.   5   ft.
158 lbs.
PRINTS—RIGHT HAN

THAYER'S INTESTINAL CASINGS, INC.
"We keep your wiener covered"
Mr. Horace Alden Thayer
c o Thayer Trust
100 Main St.
Wilkes Barre, PA 70765

No. 153964

52

Fig. 17

Doch unser Graf — was thut er itzt?
Vor ihm der todte Sohn.
Allein in seinem Zelte sitzt
Der Graf, und eine Thräne
Im Aug' auf seinen S...

Drum hangen wir so treu und warm
Am Grafen, unserm Herrn.
Allein ist er ein Heldenschwarm,
Der Donner rast in seinem Arm,
Er ist des Landes Stern.

Drum ihr dort auf... der Welt,
Die Nasen eingej...
Auch manchen ...chen Held,
Im Frieden...
Gebar...

Fig. 18

Fig. 27

Fig. 36

Fig. 44

MASSILLON, O.

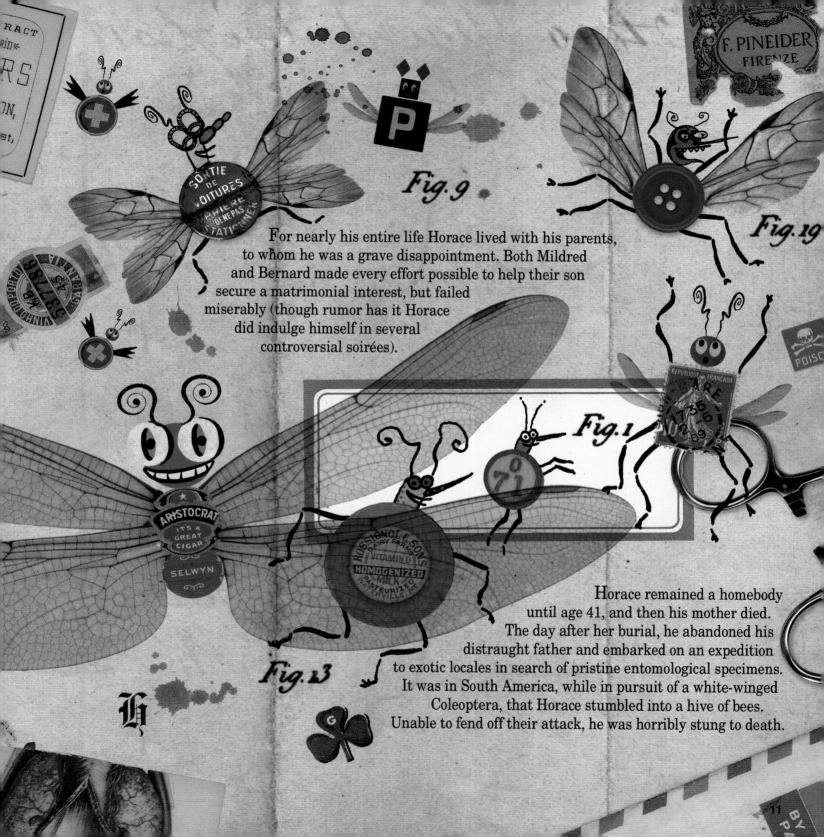

F. PINEIDER
FIRENZE

Fig. 9

Fig. 19

For nearly his entire life Horace lived with his parents, to whom he was a grave disappointment. Both Mildred and Bernard made every effort possible to help their son secure a matrimonial interest, but failed miserably (though rumor has it Horace did indulge himself in several controversial soirées).

Fig. 1

Horace remained a homebody until age 41, and then his mother died. The day after her burial, he abandoned his distraught father and embarked on an expedition to exotic locales in search of pristine entomological specimens. It was in South America, while in pursuit of a white-winged Coleoptera, that Horace stumbled into a hive of bees. Unable to fend off their attack, he was horribly stung to death.

Fig. 13

Upon news of his only child's tragic death, Bernard Minsley Thayer dropped dead of a heart attack, his estate seized, and then liquidated. Years later, a box of eccentric collages turned up on an online auction and were purchased by The Musee National d´ Naturelle in Paris at a nominal price. Annually, the museum now holds an exhibit of these very same astonishing images created from the fertile imagination of secretive artist/entomologist Horace Alden Thayer—now recognized as one of the most significant self-taught artists of the 20th century.

WHO'S AFRAID OF THE
PEPPERMINT MAN?

BY CAMILLE ROSE GARCIA

©2002 by the Prosthetic Industries Toy Company

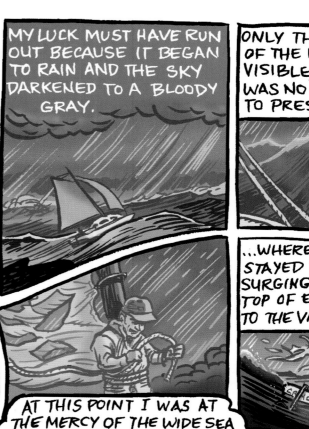

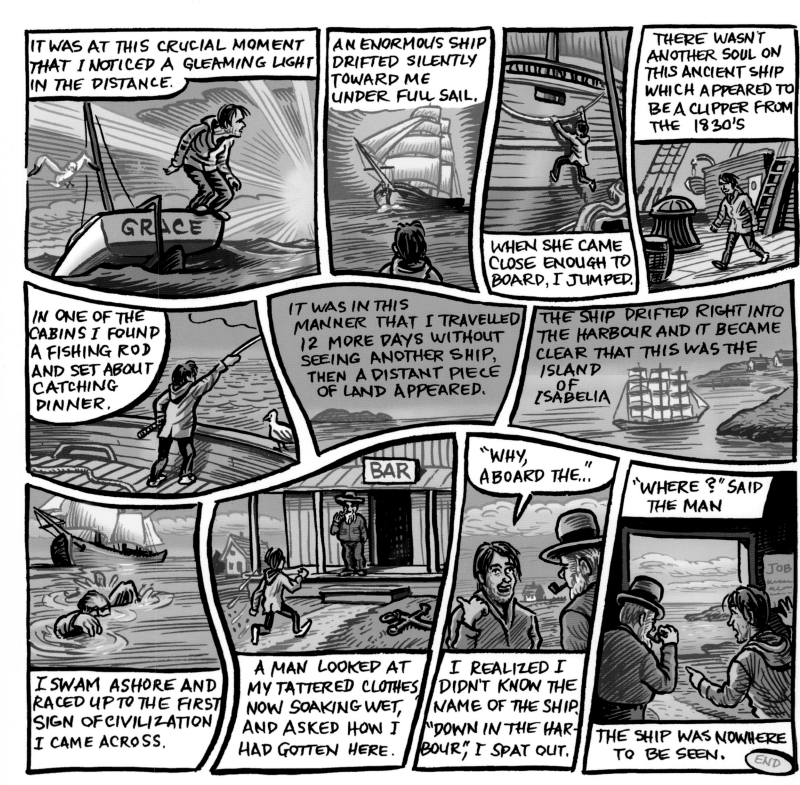

THE PAPER GRIN

STORY BY: CHARLES PAUL FREUND AND PETER HOEY
ART BY: PETER AND MARIA HOEY

THE PLACE MAKES YOU THINK IT'S A CITY, THE WEATHER REMINDS YOU OF HEAT. YOU'RE IN A PLACE THAT LOOKS JUST LIKE A PARK, ON A BENCH THAT FEELS LIKE A SEAT. IS THAT FLASH IN THE SKY A SAUCER? IS THAT THING IN YOUR HAND THE NEWS? IS THAT THOUGHT IN YOUR HEAD FROM THE STORY YOU'VE READ? OR WAS THAT A TALE THAT READ YOU?

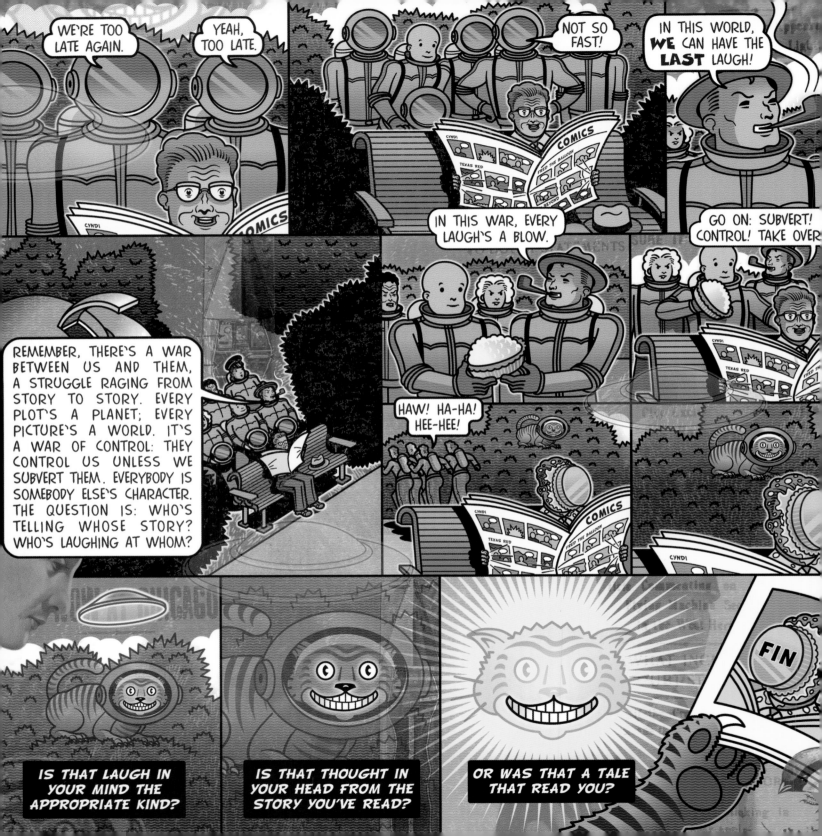

ANTS IN your PANTS in France

le Rosenthal

M. Foubar arrives in Paris.

the debonaire M. Foubar arouses no suspicion as he enters the city.

ever vigilant, M. Foubar "prends" a café at the bar.

NE POKEZ PAS!

the mercurial M. Foubar responds in flawless French.

WELL, EXCU-U-U-SEZ MOI.

ÇA, ALORS!

outf

le formidable M. Foubar.

The lone wolf, Foubar, prepares to leave the petit café.

outf

The world-weary M. Foubar feigns disinterest at the celebrities on the street.

Fou
ge

Americana

COVER COUTURE

by Monte Beauchamp

Norman Rockwell anointed him America's most gifted illustrator . . . for the *Saturday Evening Post* alone he composed nearly two hundred covers . . . as a sought-after portrait painter he accumulated the most famous of subjects—Gable, de Havilland, and Cagney, to name a few . . . *Life*, *Look*, *Ladies' Home Journal*, and *McCall's* commissioned his work . . . and while serving as a lieutenant in the Naval Reserve, he designed more than three hundred World War II recruiting posters.

For most of his professional life, John Philip Falter maintained a prodigious output of wholesome illustration and late in life was elected by his peers to the Society of Illustrators' Hall of Fame. Yet long before he was ever crowned a prince of pictures, Falter secretly toiled away in the tawdry backwaters of Depression-era pulp magazines, cranking out seedy and shocking cover portraits for *Master Detective* magazine.

But Falter did not labor alone for the publication. He was backed by yet another young genius talent—that of Dalton Stevens. Together, the two alternated front-cover slots, churning out stunning film noir–styled portraits characterized by their subjects' shocking expressions. One month's cover might showcase the face of fear, while the next that of betrayal. For nearly seven years, the two rendered magnificent portraits covering every imaginable criminal expression possible. Then suddenly, Falter fled the scene.

Several years later he resurfaced, but this time he was carving out a lucrative career with the more respectable publications. Stevens, on the other hand, drifted off into publishing obscurity, never to be heard from again.

Though they didn't live to realize it, the talented tag-team of Falter and Stevens fashioned a unique and arresting chorus line of cover portraiture for the once maligned but now celebrated throwaway pulp magazine.

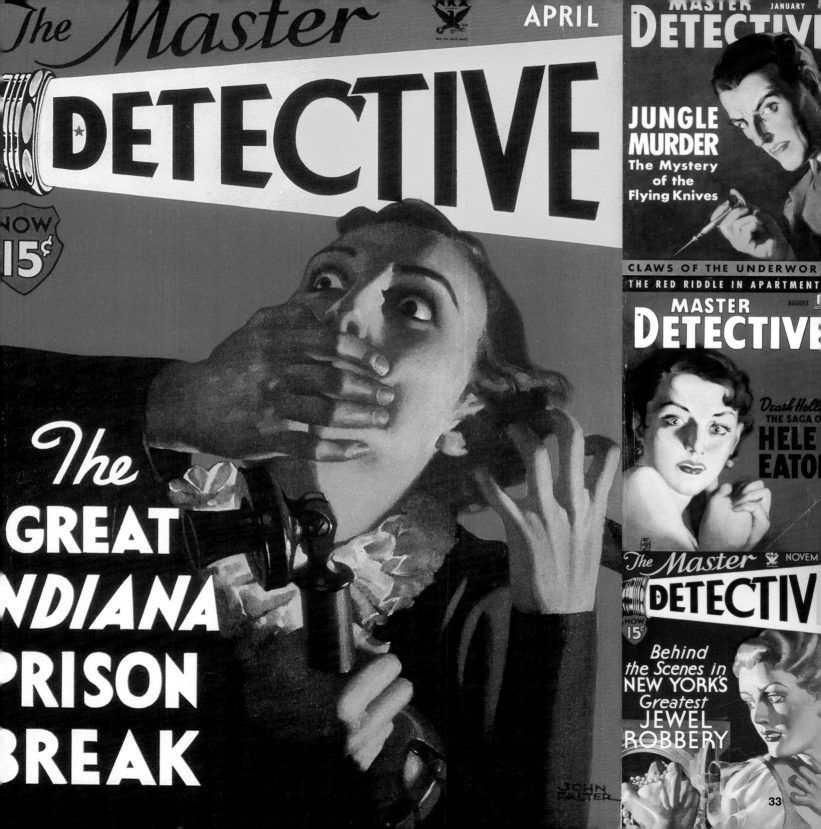

The Man With No Heart by Sue Coe

Inside, amidst piles of manure and stench, were the carcasses of 24 cows, their bones protruding through the skin, still chained in their stanchions. Calves born during the ordeal lay beside their mothers. The agent called the authorities. The police officer said he had never seen anything like it in 29 years of law enforcement. "Its totally unnacceptable to see animals die that slowly, it rips my heart out."

He was required by law to bury the cows within 72 hours. As he dragged the bodies away he avoided the neighbors. One of whom said "thats him, the man with no heart."

The End

HEY MISTER, could you PLEASE AMUSE US TO DEATH
WITH THE QUIRKY, THE STRANGE AND THE PATHETIC

All pictures, text & design considered "topical" and "newsworthy" by Jonathon Rosen

The Big Time Very Important Clowns & everybody loves a circus. Hurry! Hurry! Hurry! Step right down yes, *all the way down,* down underground for Goddamn *bread* & circus's and the comedy of a good ol' economic *meltdown* ! Who cares ? Life is **FUNNY** ! I Got a little fuck-in' horn, a horn that goes toot-toot ! Oh I am a riot. I kill me ! **You~ Forget y'little problems & worries.** C'mon in I tell ya. We got armies of mighty-ass, hyterically expensive **military computers**

of harpys screaming diva level siren songs, disheveled songs of useless information, designed not for your imagination

and it's gonna entertain you to **Death** ! The fad for you is OVER my friend ! Check it out, OUT ! Heh, heh-Hey ! There goes the imagination… Why, where did it go ?!? Because you silly clown, We Can have it NOW ! We can get 5 of you to work on somethin' that in the end only one person actually gets Paid for ! **You with your old fashioned** [continues top of next page]

crunching numbers, crushing, mutilating, transforming funny little numbers by the bucketfull into

a major plumbing nightmare

VANITY INDUSTRIES

PRESS AND PUBLICITY

MARKETING DESIRE

SOCIAL LUBRICANT

DEBASED SOUL MANURE

TRIED & TRUE

RAGING HORMONES

INSOMNIA SOLUTIONS

FAKE COLLECTOR'S ITEM

CUT OUT BIN

DEAD END

SOUL…USELESS. STUPID ! HA HA ! We can download 20 guys into a little ittty-bitty car with our new circus 5.2 while you idiot, while YOU Still want to want do things by hand…BY HAND…BAH ! Plus you cost too MUCH ! We live on AIR & INFLATED STOCKS MY BACKWARD thinking UN-FUNNY FRIEND ! Heh, Heh !

TIGHT ROPE WALKERS. YOU KNOW YOU WANT TO BE THERE WHEN THEY FALL.

I LOVE ME

CASHED IN STOCKS

We got the bread, we got the circuses, we got the Anna-Nicole-Lobotomy-Smith for fuck's sake. What more diversion do you want ? How many creative guys does the world need, anyway ? Creative, don't we have enough space filling, anesthetizing stuff already ? I'm an image bank ! Wheeeeeeeeeeeeeeeeeeeeeeee ! New stuff, HONK, New stuff, Honk….Oh you sad sad clown. Why the sad face and the poor expression ? Miss your pent-house, the jaguar the place in the country the free trips to Barbados ? The cocaine ? Oh there you go, that again sniveling. whining

again about your precious SOUL for crissakes. GET OVER IT ! It's OBSOLETE DO YOU HEAR ME ? Toot toot ! Oh, I am a riot. Oh, here come my fellow clowns oh this is gonna be good get outta my way you sniveling bastard ! Sing it gates, 'OB-SO-LETE, OB-SO-LETE, O you are so OB-SO-LETE' ! I Know, let's have a war ! Clowns, line up! I AM YOUR COMMANDER-in-Hanker-CHIEF ! ATTENTION ! Shoot the enemy, kill the other clowns, shoot the dancing bear, kill the trapeze artists, kill the artists and the band and the ring-leader and the lions and the monkeys and tigers and elephants and oh my yes we don't need 'em cause we can get anything we want for free on the damn phosphorescent screen ya sniveling moron ! toot toot ! Oh I am a riot. The END, Absolutely.

ABSOLUTE POWER. CORRUPTS ABSOLUTELY.

MANUFACTURING DESIRE, EMPTY SOCIAL LUBRICANT.

dirty girl ®
body language

happy,   pleased,

spilling over

with
girly glee

Tarantula B...

Art: Walter Minus.
Story: Laurent Bouhnik.

58

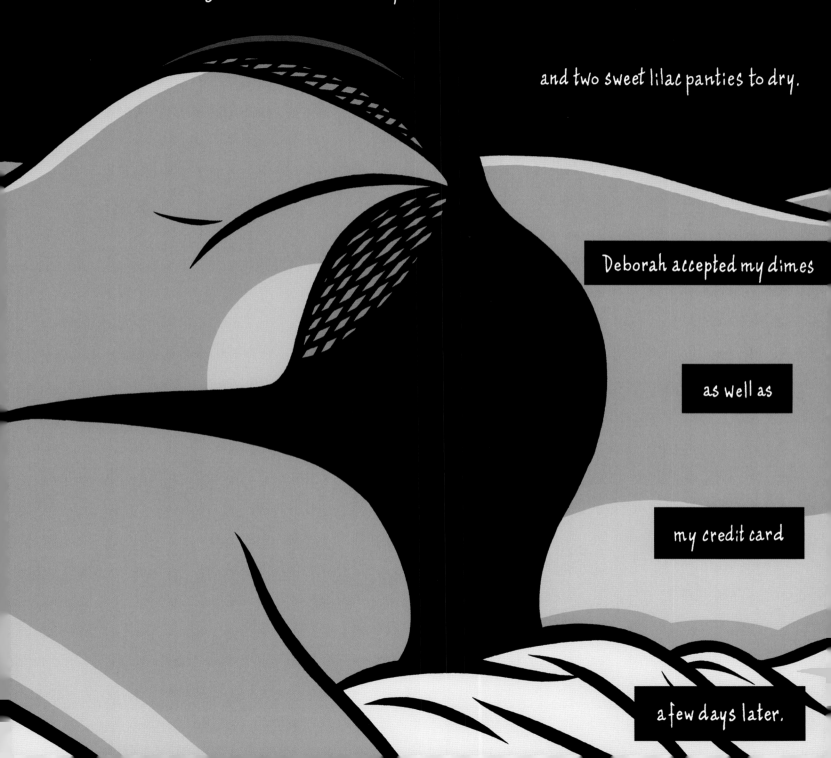

I was exposing my dirty clothes at the laundromat.
She was short on change and still had her baby dolls

and two sweet lilac panties to dry.

Deborah accepted my dimes

as well as

my credit card

a few days later.

After walking Lillie, her one-eyed
chihuahua, I barely had time to push
the vaccum around, change the tank water
for her fish, wash the windows
and water the plants before

she

awoke.

61

Losing my job as an accountant finally gave me the time to repair her roof and plant some trees in the garden.

Georgette, the pharmacist's wife,
gave me sewing and French cuisine lessons.
At the same time, she would lick my wounds
and apply different brands of arnica cream.
Deborah was a little upset
for being late with the pool
that I worked on every evening

for
her.

But she didn't harbor any hard feelings.

Deborah liked that I parked myself in her garage, so I could paint the Ford Mustang she worshiped

in lilac.

MY COLD WAR

TEXT AND ART: SPAIN

I WAS BORN IN 1940 AND MY MEMORIES OF WORLD WAR II ARE STILL VIVID. I REMEMBER HEARING ABOUT COMMUNIST LED STRIKES AND ALTHOUGH THE REDS WERE ALWAYS SPOKEN OF IN OMINOUS TONES I FORMED AN OPINION OF THEM, SEEMINGLY ON MY OWN, AS GOOD GUYS FIGHTING FOR THE COMMON PEOPLE

© SPAIN RODRIGUEZ '02

THE WAR HAD BEEN OVER FOR LESS THAN A YEAR WHEN WINSTON CHURCHILL GAVE HIS SPEECH IN FULTON, MISSOURI, ATTACKING OUR FORMER ALLY, THE SOVIET UNION. WHEN I TRIED TO GET MY DAD'S ATTENTION, HE JUST SAID...

LISTEN!

UH: DAD?

..FROM STETTIN ON THE BALTIC TO TRIESTE IN THE ADRIATIC, AN IRON CURTAIN HAS DESCENDED ACROSS THE CONTINENT.

OF COURSE I DIDN'T KNOW THAT CHURCHILL HAD STOLEN THE TERM "IRON CURTAIN" FROM NAZI PROPAGANDA MINISTER JOSEF GOEBBELS. I STILL HAD A CHILD'S COMPLETE FAITH IN THE ADULT WORLD, BUT STILL I WONDERED...

HOW COULD ANYONE BUILD AN IRON WALL ALL THE WAY ACROSS EUROPE?

MY DAD HAD DISMISSED CHURCHILL'S SPEECH AS "POLITICS". BUT IN THE NEXT FEW YEARS THINGS BEGAN TO HEAT UP. I REMEMBER HIM AND MY COUSIN, WHO HAD BEEN IN THE AIR FORCE IN WW II, LOOKING AT ONE OF MY BLACKHAWK COMICS.

THEY REALLY WANT A WAR. YOU CAN EVEN SEE IT IN THESE COMIC BOOKS.

ONE OF THE STORIES WAS ABOUT A SMALL NATION BEING INVADED BY A LARGER COUNTRY NAMED "RUSHAGA".

ABOUT THIS TIME A CHANGE IN ATTITUDE CAME OVER ME. I HAD COMPLETELY FORGOTTEN MY EARLIER IMPRESSIONS OF COMMUNISTS. (MY ATTENTION SPAN ON THESE ISSUES WAS ABOUT 35 SECONDS.)

WHY DO WORKERS THINK THEY HAVE A RIGHT TO STRIKE? ITS CLEAR THAT FACTORY OWNERS SHOULD BE FREE TO DO WHATEVER THEY WANT WITH THEIR OWN PROPERTY.

LIKE MY EARLIER ATTITUDES, I HAVE NO MEMORY OF ANY ADULT INFLUENCE. TO MYSELF THEY SEEMED LIKE ORIGINAL IDEAS. THE FACT THAT I WOULD SOON BE ONE OF THE WORKERS THAT I LOOKED DOWN ON NEVER OCCURED TO ME.

THE PROPAGANDA WAR GREW IN INTENSITY. IN ONE ANTICOMMUNIST SHORT, A MAN WAKES UP ONE SUNDAY MORNING TO FIND HIS KIDS RADICALLY CHANGED.

C'MON, KIDS. TIME FOR MASS!

RELIGION IS THE OPIATE OF THE PEOPLE, DAD.

BETTER THAN MASS, THE MASSES FREE OF SUPERSTITION

FEAR OF AN ACTUAL SOVIET INVASION WAS IN THE AIR AND I HAD DREAMS OF THE RUSSIANS LANDING ON LAKE ERIE AND INVADING BUFFALO.

AFTER THE WAR WE HAD SEEMED INVINCIBLE. WHEN I ASKED MY DAD HOW THE RUSSIANS COULD JUST COME IN AND TAKE US OVER, HE DIDN'T ANSWER.

THE FATHER OF ONE OF THE KIDS AT MY SCHOOL WAS CALLED BEFORE HUAC (THE HOUSE UNAMERICAN ACTIVITIES COMMITTEE). I WAS TOLD NOT TO SAY HELLO TO HIM.

UH, HI, BOBBY.

THE COMMUNISTS WERE VERY CLEVER AT MANIPULATING YOUNG MINDS. MY MOM SHOWED ME A PRIME EXAMPLE.

LOOK! THEY'RE SAYING IT'S BAD TO BE AGAINST COMMUNISTS.

...BUT SHE DID SAVE ALL MY E.C. COMICS.

IN 1950 THE U.S. INTERVENED TO KEEP KOREANS FROM COMMITTING ACTS OF AGGRESSION AGAINST THEMSELVES. I WAS GLAD. AT LAST WE WERE GOING TO SHOW THOSE COMMIES WHO WAS BOSS.

THE "POLICE ACTION" AS IT WAS CALLED, WAS VIVIDLY PORTRAYED IN COMIC BOOKS AS IT DRAGGED ON TO A STALEMATE.

WHEN I GOT OLDER I READ A BOOK CALLED "THE SHARK AND THE SARDINES" BY JOSE AREVALO, THE FIRST ELECTED PRESIDENT OF GUATEMALA THE SECOND FREELY ELECTED PRESIDENT, JACOBO ARBENZ, WAS OUSTED IN A U.S.-SPONSORED COUP AMID MUCH ANTI-COMMUNIST HOOPLA.

THE BOOK DETAILS AMERICAN INTERVENTION IN LATIN AMERICA ON BEHALF OF CORRUPT REGIMES THAT WOULD BE LABELED AGGRESSION IF DONE BY ANYONE ELSE. THE U.S. BACKED REGIME IN GUATEMALA BEGAN A BLOODY REIGN OF TERROR THAT LASTS TO THIS DAY.

NEARLY A DECADE LATER, THE U.S. GOVERNMENT TRIED TO PREVENT ANOTHER PEOPLE FROM COMMITTING "AGGRESSION" AGAINST THEMSELVES. THE VIETNAM WAR BEGAN WITH A HOAX - THE TONKIN GULF INCIDENT...

...AND ENDED WITH A HOAX - THE MYTH OF THE P.O.W.-MIAS.

I WENT TO THE SOVIET UNION IN 1987. I WAS IMPRESSED WITH ITS LACK OF FREE EXPRESSION. AN EDITOR I MET SHOWED ME A COPY OF NEWSWEEK AS IF IT WAS CHILD PORNOGRAPHY.

THERE WAS NEVER ANY POSSIBILITY THAT AMERICA COULD BE TAKEN OVER BY RUSSIA OR ANYONE ELSE, BUT THE "DEFENCE" BUILD UP, IN ONE OF THE BIGGEST EVER "SOCIALISM-FOR-THE-RICH" SCAMS, PUT BILLIONS INTO THE POCKETS OF FAT CATS.

Amber Eyes

(Scandinavian folk tale) — transcribed by Richard Sala

①

BURIED TREASURE

No Trespassing

3

4

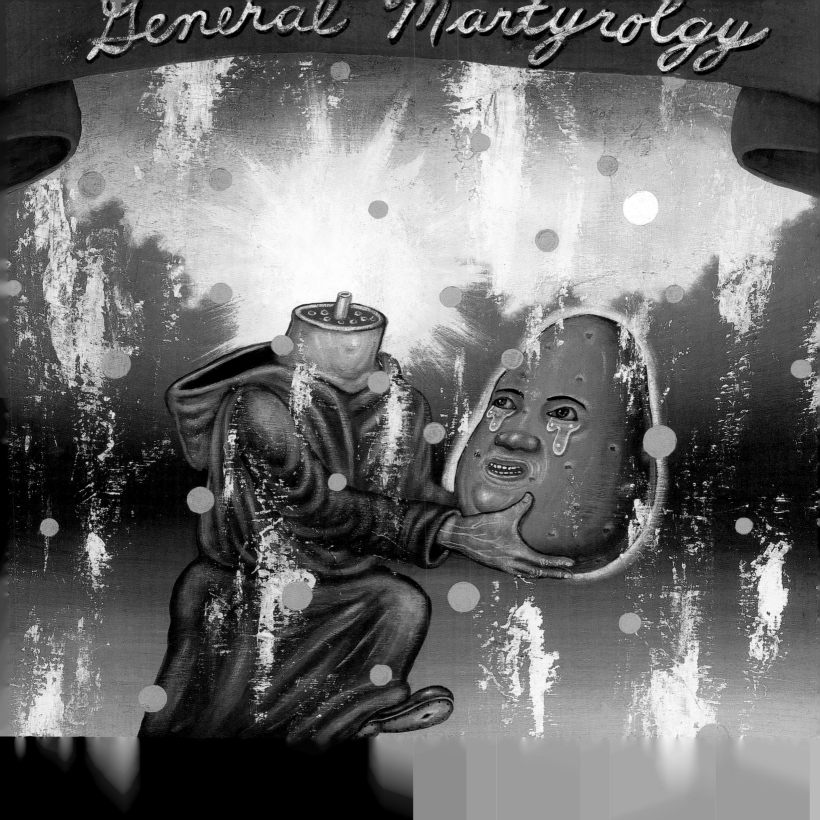

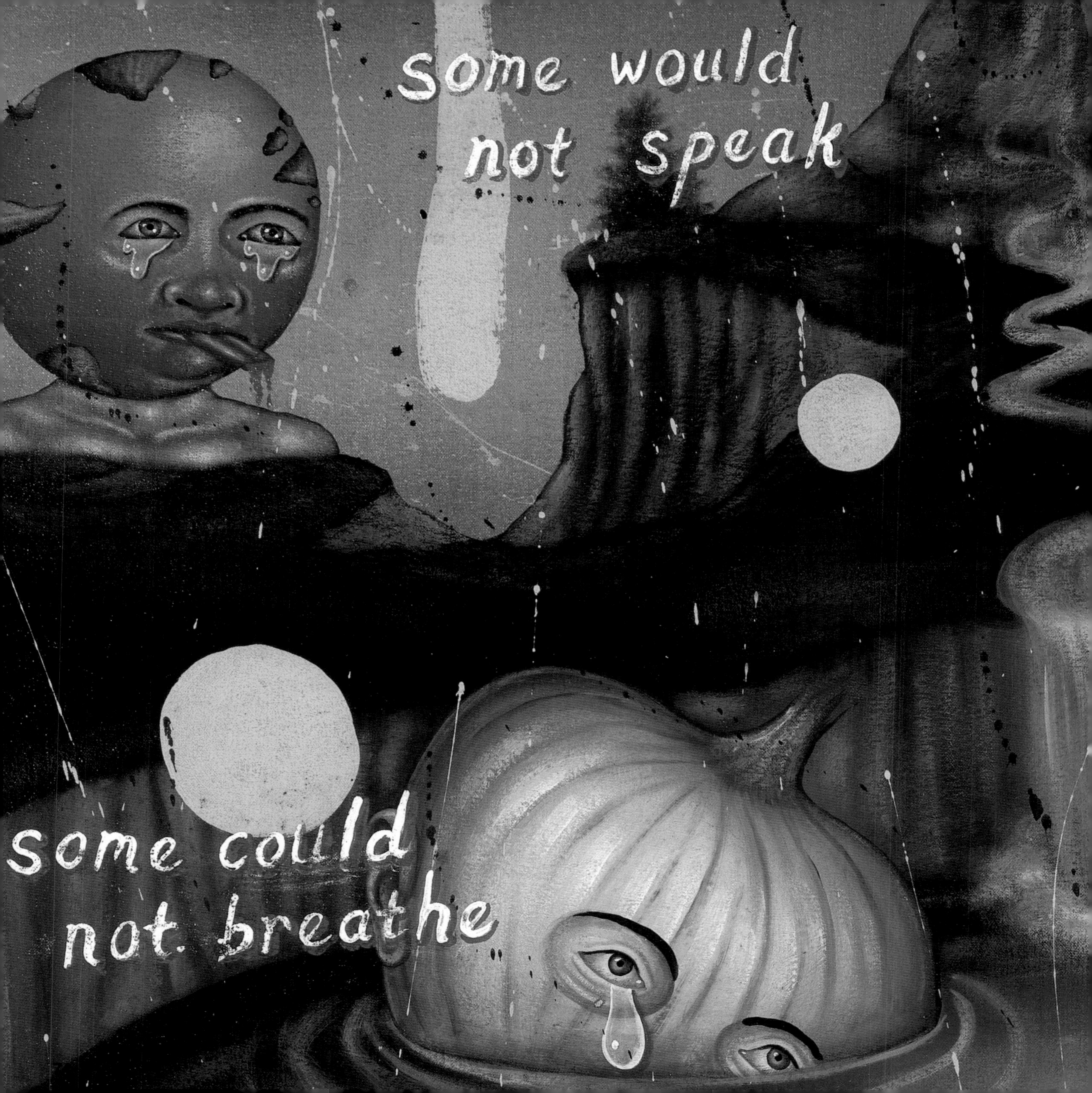
some would
not speak
some could
not breathe

some lost all feeling

some lost the ability to think

BIX and TRAM

BIX BEIDERBECKE · WITH FRANKIE · TRUMBAUER'S ORCHESTRA

SET C-144 · A HOT JAZZ CLASSIC · #20 IN A SERIES THAT

COLUMBIA RECORDS

copyright, 1947, columbia records inc.

A TRIBUTE to JIM FLORA!

Contains his hit '50s album cover art *Bix and Tram*, *Mambo for Cats*, *Redskin Romp*, and many more!

RCA VICTOR
RECORDS

THIS IS
BENNY
GOODMAN
and his
ORCHESTRA

CHANGES
CAMEL HOP
SWINGTIME IN THE ROCKIES
SUGARFOOT STOMP
BIG JOHN SPECIAL
LIFE GOES TO A PARTY
RIFFIN' AT THE RITZ
WRAPPIN' IT UP

LPT-3056

RCA VICTOR
LJM-1004

A HIGH FIDELITY RECORDING

shorty rogers
courts the
count

JUMP FOR ME
TOPSY
IT'S SAND, MAN
BASIE EYES
DOGGIN' AROUND
DOWN FOR DOUBLE
OVER AND OUT
H & J
TAPS MILLER
TICKLETOE
SWINGIN' THE BLUES
WALK, DON'T RUN

83

RCA VICTOR
LM-1891
RED SEAL

RICHARD STRAUSS

TILL EULENSPIEGEL

DEATH AND TRANSFIGURATION

TOSCANINI • NBC SYMPHONY ORCHESTRA

85

Mambo For CATS

RCA VICTOR
45EP EPB-1063

A "NEW ORTHOPHONIC" HIGH FIDELITY RECORDING

COLLABORATION

SHORTY ROGERS

ANDRE PREVIN

Flora

© RCA Printed in U S A

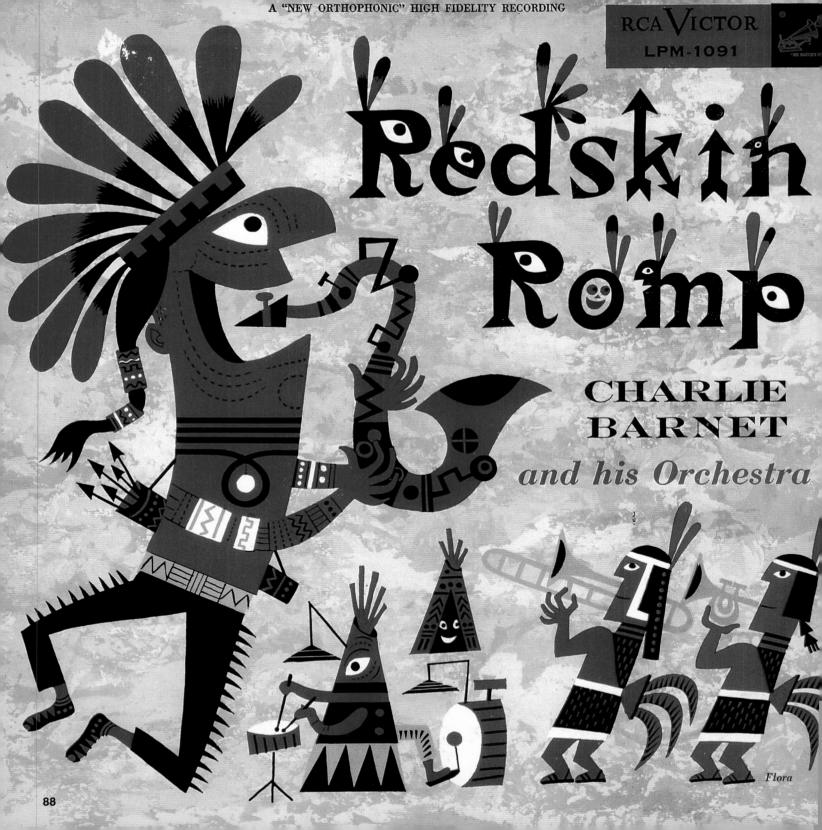

FETAL ELVIS!

Somewhere in the backwoods of Tupelo, Mississippi, you'll find a special young embryo! No ordinary collection of dividing cells, he is...

Yes, it's another thrill-packed adventure starring that wily fetus, FETAL ELVIS and his buddy, Sid of the Loyal White Corpuscles!

by Mark Landman

A carefree day in the womb is shattered when Fetal Elvis makes a shocking discovery!

Muh GEE-TAR, it's gone!

Whoa! And someone left a funky old accordion in it's place!

Look Boss, a note! It's BLACKMAIL!

Ifin you want yer guitar back, Yuh has to KISS ME! Meet me at midnite in the left ventricle. signed, A GURL

YAWN! It's jes' anuther STOOPID GIRL who wants my hot lil' bod...

Why ARE all the girls so crazy about you, Boss?

Them wimmen is all crazy about me 'cause I don't give a DAMN about them! Matter of fact, I think they is kinda "icky"!

Wow, you sure are a smooth operator, Boss!

Thas right! I'm jes' gonna TAKE my gee-tar back and WHOMP this stoopid girl right on the haid! Kiss? HAH!

Yee-haw!

That night, Fetal Elvis sneaks past his mentor and guardian, Colonel Placenta!

RACING NEWS
Secretariat gets lucky

Good thing I still got that map of the fo'bidden regions I done STOLT last time I snuck out!

And so the brave (if exceedingly stupid) little fetus begins his journey, fighting treacherous arterial currents...

Avoiding the constant threat of the dreaded Anti-Body Police and their killer T-Cells...

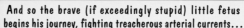

And of course, making a short stop in the bile duct to "refresh his do"...

Dang this stuff sure makes my hair shine all pretty-like!

Finally arriving at his destination- the left ventricle of the Host Mother's heart!

Thank Gawd I made it, I'm just about outta Percodans!

Now where is that stoopid girl anyway? I aim tuh gonna WHOMP her a good...

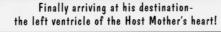

...one

Hi Y'all!

Ah'm Fetal Kitten!

Omigosh, I done never felt like THIS before!

The helpless fetus is totally besotted with lust!

Thas a good job! You kin do mah other boot next!

Sob! I expect I should feel all degraded and such...

Suddenly, Fetal Elvis is ambushed by Monocytes!

Git him, Boys!

Fetal Elvis receives a terrible beating, mercifully lapsing into unconsciousness...

Gosh, this must be what they call "Rough Sex"!

...only to awaken, kidnapped and securely bound!

Welcome to the lower colon, Sugar!

Ah appreciate the excitin' sex, Ms. Kitten, but muh hair is gittin' all messed up...

When suddenly, an ominous figure emerges from the shadows...

WE'LL MESS UP MORE THAN YOUR HAIR, PRETTY BOY!

OH NO! It's Evil Jesse, muh evil twin brother! I'm righteously screwed now!

Evil?!? HAH!

The realization that

any day, at any moment,

these bombs could wipe us off the map with the push of a button has shadowed me in daydreams and nightmares since that time.

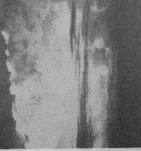
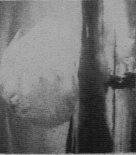

Russia has a similar number of strategic weapons with approximately 2000 on hair-trigger alert.

Although I'll never stop worrying and learn to love the bomb, it has certainly motivated me to wake up and smell the roses, see the world, not sweat the small stuff, and bla,bla,bla. Because if we are poised to be blown to smithereens,

it always begs the question...

The U.S. currently has 2000 intercontinental land-based bombs, 3456 nuclear weapons on submarines minutes from their targets and 1750 nuclear weapons on intercontinental planes.

Fat Man-type bomb

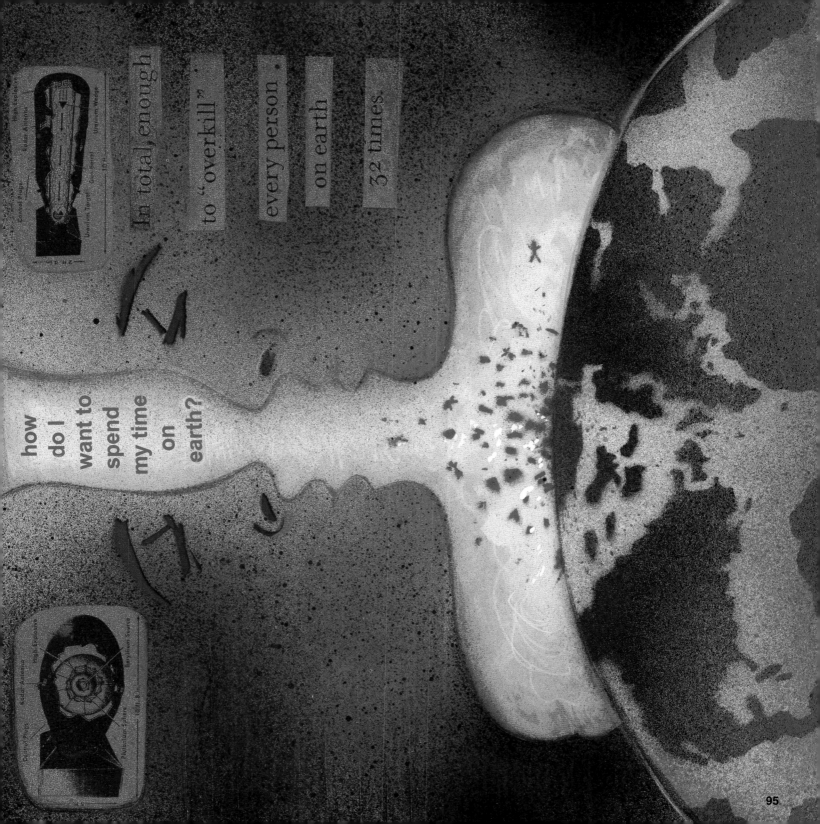

In total, enough to "overkill" every person · on earth 3² times.

how do I want to spend my time on earth?

GETTING

New & Used! Go!

CHRONICLE BOOKS • SAN FRANCISCO

EDITED & DESIGNED BY MONTE BEAUCHAMP

Thank you: Jim Heimann, for bringing this project to the attention of Chronicle Books. A very special thanks to: Alan Rapp, for his editorial guidance, good taste, and great ideas; Leslie Davisson, for editorial assistance; Sara Schneider, for design support and coordination; and Steve Kim, for production coordination. With deep gratitude, thank you: Doug Allen, Mark Alvarado, Gary Baseman, Stephane Blanquet, Laurent Bouhnik, Irwin Chusid, Greg Clarke, The Clayton Brothers, Sue Coe, Douglas Fraser, Charles Freund, Drew Friedman, Camille Rose Garcia, David Goldin, Gary Groth, Matti Hagelberg, Becky Hall, Doug Hawk, Jukka Heiskanen, Peter and Maria Hoey, Jem and Scout, Haley Johnson, Peter Kuper, Mark Landman, Walter Minus, Mark Mothersbaugh, Teresa Mucha, Christian Northeast, Eric Reynolds, Jonathon Rosen, Marc Rosenthal, Mark Ryden, Richard Sala, Spain, Jeffrey Steele, Fred Stonehouse, and Kim Thompson.

Designed, Edited, and Produced by: Monte Beauchamp

10 9 8 7 6 5 4 3 2 1

Chronicle Books LLC, 85 Second Street, San Francisco, California 94105. www.chroniclebooks.com

CONTENTS

INTRODUCTION

In a lot of ways, how *BLAB!* ever got started is *way* beyond me. It was a fluke! One of those things you do in life born of an earlier influence, which in turn takes on a life of its own.

What I do recall is that *BLAB!* began in 1985 as a response to my despair over feeling trapped in the dysfunctional world of corporate advertising. To help counter that despair, my wife at the time suggested I draw a comic book, something in which to channel my frustration.

When I was a sophomore in high school living in a small river town in the Midwest, a chance exposure to *Zap Comix*—just one of a new breed of comic books that had begun streaming out of San Francisco's counterculture in the late 1960s—blew my young mind! These "comix" were so out there that I just had to find out what made their artists tick. What I soon discovered was that most were still grinding an ax over the censoring of their beloved *Tales from the Crypt*, *Weird Science*, and the rest of the EC line of comics from the days when they were all kids.

So in the mid-1980s—nearly a decade and a half later—I set out to document their EC experience and contacted these artists to see if they would "blab" about it in a one-shot, self-published fanzine. And the rest, as they say, is history . . .

When word arrived that Chronicle wanted to do this book, a sense of pride washed over me. I began to reflect just how much *BLAB!* had grown. And then moments later, I realized something: *BLAB!* never would have happened had it not been for that difficult time in advertising taking place in my life. But for which now I am forever grateful.

—*Monte Beauchamp, Chicago*

GETTING

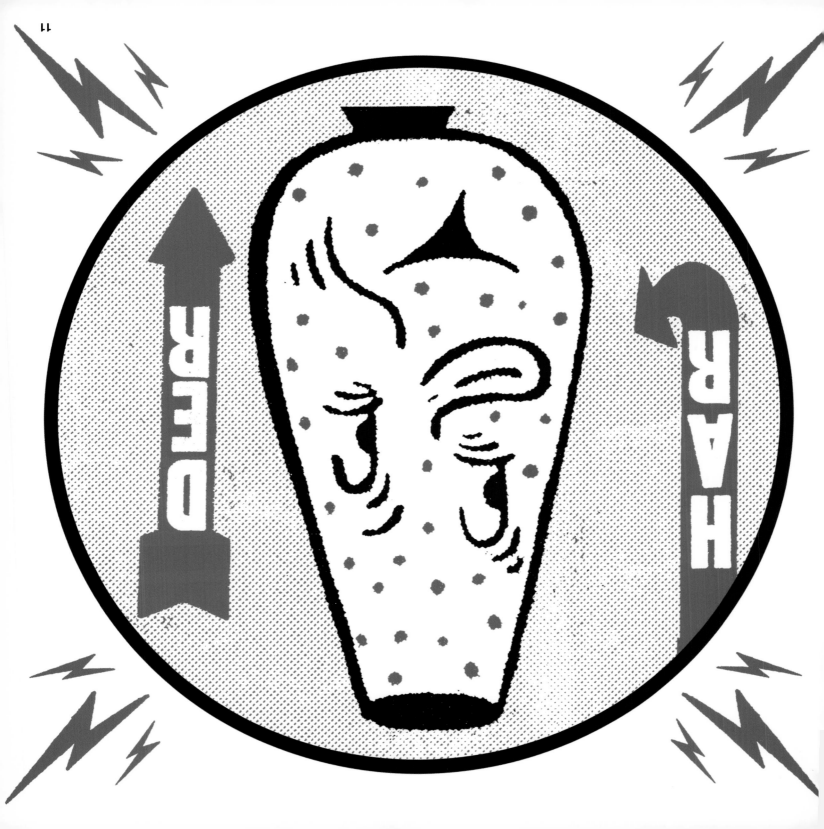

GOOD DOG book

Then one morning at God's
Birthday party, God said, "Carl,
would you like to walk my dog
snowball?" "OH YES!" Carl replied.
but God, I would love to keep
Snowball all to my own."

Stood all alone. He was an
extremely quiet child.

GOOD BOY!

Carl and Madonna Snowball

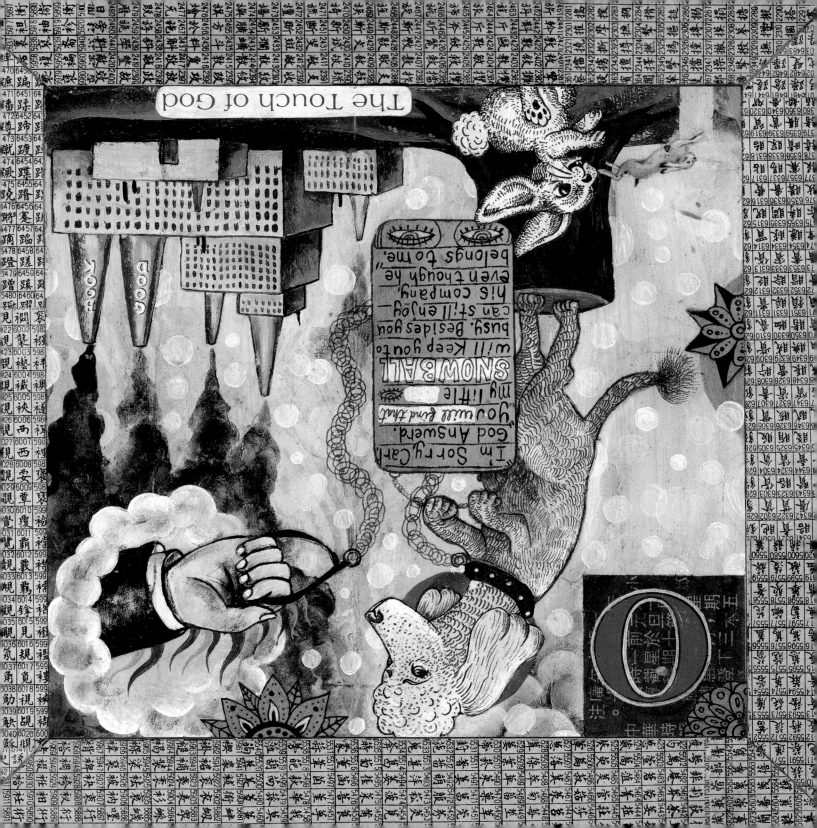

SUNDAY

Carl found that no one wanted bibles so Carl decided that to have that SNOWBALL, he would have to CHEAT. He hid all the bibles in the big OAK tree.

GOD was very pleased, not knowing what Carl did with the Bible. He was just glad to have gotten rid of so many of them. Thank you God, kind and good. What you DONT know won't HURT you. Carl

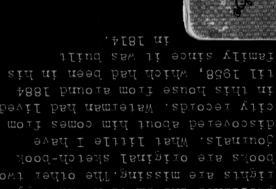

WATERMAN MOSES
by David Goldin

I first discovered the work of Waterman Moses in the attic of a run-down Victorian in Providence, Rhode Island. I was helping to renovate the place when I stumbled upon five of Waterman's books. Three are printed, but the publisher information and copyrights are missing. The other two books are original sketch-book journals. What little I have discovered about him comes from city records. Waterman had lived in this house from around 1884 till 1958, which had been in his family since it was built in 1814.

I have searched for more of his work over the years and have found barely a word about him—anywhere! Several old newspaper articles mention an exhibition in London of Waterman's work, a set designed for an opera in Prague, and a bicycle race in the south of France.

He also traveled among some of the finer social circles in Newport and New York, according to his journals. I discovered one reference from an interview with Saul Steinberg. The interviewer inquired how Steinberg had received a black eye. To which he replied, "Waterman, the bastard!!!".

ARTWORK: ©2001 Julien Mandel. TRANSLATION: Kim Thompson

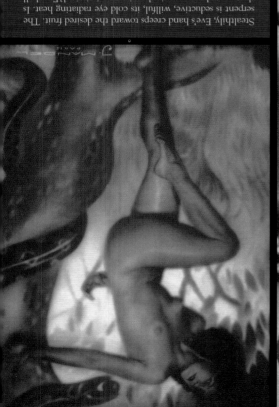

Stealthily, Eve's hand creeps toward the desired fruit. The serpent is seductive, willful, its cold eye radiating heat. Is she tempted or mesmerized, curious or victimized? Eve shall taste the venom-filled apple, but it will condemn her to an endless quest. Will she find fulfillment in these moonlit games? Can she merge in harmony with a being that will never complete her? Is she not giving herself to a shadow?

MIS FANTASTIQUES

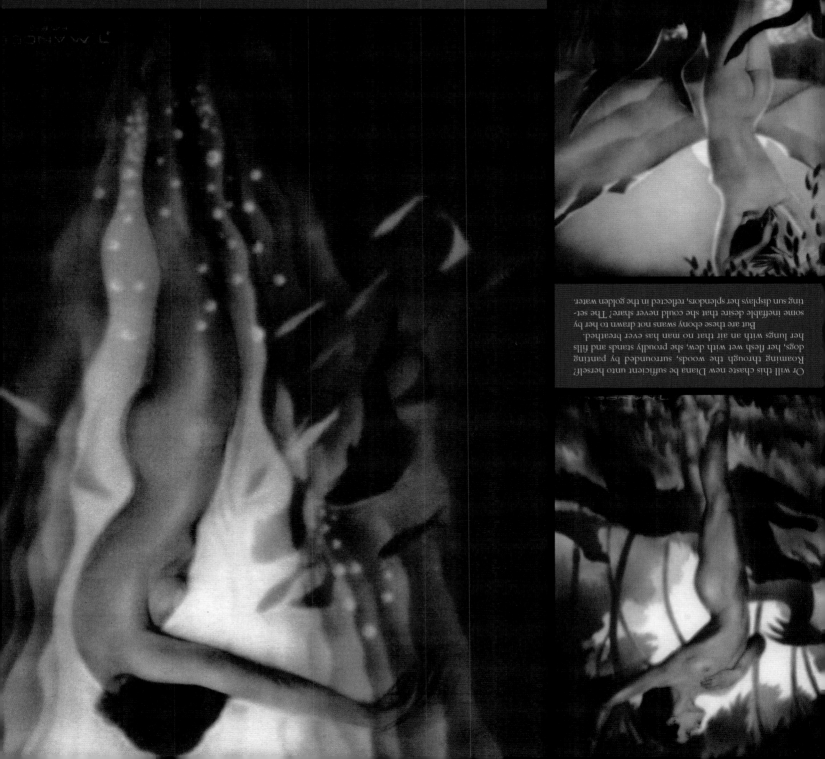

One of the swans is bolder than the rest... Does it take liberties with her, as did once the King of Gods with Leda, thus proving that even a swan should be looked at with suspicion, were it to thrust itself upon one?

Perhaps she should seek to appease her fever in a different element... In the palm of her hand, the fountain brings her a voluptuous sensation of cool liquidity... Like a heavy arrow, she then plunges deep, amidst the currents, the bubbles and the fish, lovers of a strange kind, plentiful and timid.

Or will this chaste new Diana be sufficient unto herself? Roaming through the woods, surrounded by panting dogs, her flesh wet with dew, she proudly stands and fills her lungs with an air that no man has ever breathed.

But are these ebony swans not drawn to her by some ineffable desire that she could never share? The setting sun displays her splendors, reflected in the golden water.

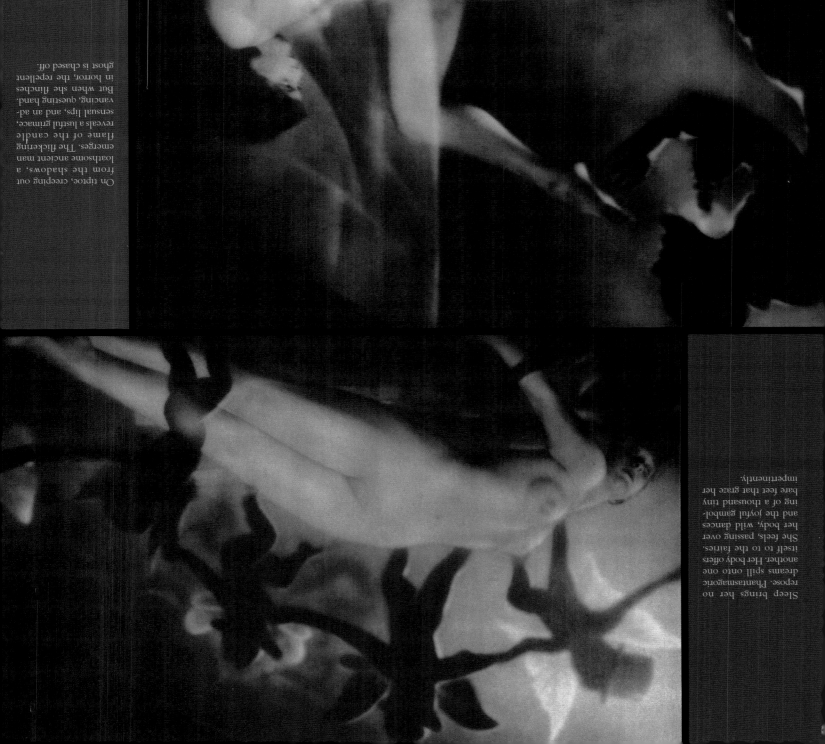

On tiptoe, creeping out from the shadows, a loathsome ancient man emerges. The flickering flame of the candle reveals a lustful grimace, sensual lips, and an advancing, questing hand. But when she flinches in horror, the repellent ghost is chased off.

Sleep brings her no repose. Phantasmagoric dreams spill onto one another. Her body offers itself to the fairies. She feels, passing over her body, wild dances and the joyful gamboling of a thousand tiny bare feet that graze her impertinently.

She is paralyzed by fear ... Her dream multiplies her terrors. Now she has been drawn into some sort of blazing jungle. Next to an implacable yet fiery-eyed tiger, she marches dumbly, toward some unknown new torture...

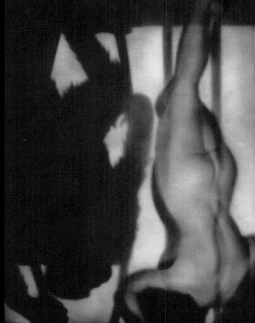

Suddenly, a shift ... The torment of the spider, which promised to be lengthy, is succeeded by this unequal battle in the cage of a roaring lion. She focuses all her remaining energy into her stiffened arms, advancing on the predator... Exhausted now, she leans against the wall, helpless prey to a gigantic gorilla, which effortlessly bends apart the iron bars to seize her...

Finally, she is cast down a stone staircase into oblivion, and regains consciousness only to behold a giant, ravenous bear seeking to crush her in its claws...

After these manifold terrors provoked by fierce beasts, her fear redoubles as she is stalked by the cruelest, the most devious, the most perverse of creatures—Man, in the throes of passion! A moment's respite fails to soothe her... Her fearful imagination pushes her to seek out new violent emotions...

MANDEL
PARIS

An unknown figure proposes to drag her down to Hell. Won't her sick curiosity find enough to satisfy her in this mysterious domain? She can't resist…

Along the walls of the moist grottoes, flickering lights illuminate the profiles of demons. And suddenly the Serpent, her first seductor, thrusts in her direction a long and forked tongue.

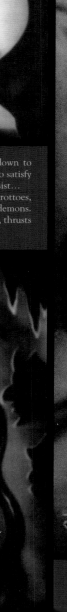

J. MANDEL
PARIS

Amidst a whirlwind of black birds, she comes to believe that she too is taking flight… A pale star bathes the infinite clouds in a sinister luminescence. With a great beating of wings, the darkling birds weave in and out of each other's paths, endlessly.

A fantastic landscape then appears. Walls, turrets, infernal belltowers, painted red by the enormous crescent of the moon… Demons clambering up to where a terrified Eve stands.

The hellish dance spins out of control… Cloven feet, hooked hands, horned foreheads: a terrifying sabbath, from which she can see no escape…

A stronger light attracts her and then dazzles her… And now it is an infinity of bats that flits around her, their thousand delicate grazings of her skin provoking uncontrollable shivers…

A passage avails Eve naught… It soon ends in an inferno, surrounded by the sordid scrabbling of contorted witches and hideous monsters…

Without respite, she is pursued by contorted faces, by infernal laughter, by unwavering stares and avid lips… Viscous arms seize her, nails claw at her…

She is overwhelmed by utter despair… She feels that there is no way out, and the hellish satyrs who are about to seize her continue to circle tirelessly about.

Then she believes that she will surely die, overlooked during her solitary death throes by a macabre being whose glacial hand rests upon her knee.

And then it is suddenly as if a renewal has taken place… like a mad dash to the light, toward which she is being pulled by benevolent and athletic young genies…

And finally the horrible night is at an end, and the warm rays of the sun spill onto the newly becalmed Eve and gently erase

Gruss Vom Krampus!

In nineteenth-century Germany, legend had it that those who were pure of heart bore witness to the magic of Christmas Eve. Some saw rivers turn to wine. Others heard animals speak. Mountains supposedly opened, revealing precious gems deep within. Church bells clanged from the depths of an icy Baltic sea and barren trees bloomed, bearing fruit on this cold December night.

The following morning, children of goodwill sprang from their beds and rushed to the shoes they had placed by the chimney the night before. Inside they'd discover treats left for them by jolly ol' Saint Nicholas . . . and joy would fill the air.

Disobedient children, however, awoke to the shakes and the shivers. In their shoes awaited switches, with which their parents would spank them. Or worse yet, they'd be paid a visit by the Krampus.

In European folklore, the Krampus is Saint Nicholas's dark servant—a hairy, horned supernatural beast whose pointed ears and long slithering tongue gave misbehavers the creeps!

The Krampus terrorized the bad until they promised to be good. Some he spanked. Others he whipped. And a few he shackled, stuffed in his large wooden basket, then hurled into the flames of Hell!

Such scenarios were delineated by skilled and imaginative Old World craftsmen, printed on penny postcards and disseminated throughout Europe. The rare examples that follow are, perhaps, the best history has left to offer.

—*Monte Beauchamp*

Üdvözlet a Krampusztól

Gruß vom Krampus

Gruss vom Krampus

Gruss vom Krampus

Gruss vom Krampus

Gruss vom Krampus

Gruß vom Krampus

Gruss vom Krampus!

Gruß vom Krampus

Mit dem Korbe auf dem Rücken, Ruth' und Kette in der Hand
Sucht der rothe Krampus die schlimmen Kinder in dem Land;
Doch zu den Braven geht er niemals, d'rum merk Dir dieses Bildchen
Sei immer fromm und folgsam und vor dem Ungethüm auf der Hut.

Den schwarzen Krampus sieh mal an!
Wie der Racker hauen kann!
Doch seine Ruthe brennt und sticht
Nur schlimme Kinder — brave nicht.
Die Schlimmen zähneklappern d'rum,
Wenn Krampus geht im Lande um.

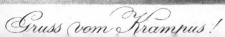

Gruss vom Krampus!

Gruss vom Krampus.

Gruss vom Krampus

Gruß vom KRAMPUS

Üdvözlet a Krampusztól!

ectoplasmic
intoxican
〈enema〉:

incubus

36

A CASE

THAT ISN'T DELIRIUM TREMENS AFFLICTING THE

OF

STAFFS AND PATRONS OF SEVERAL INFAMOUS BARS—

THE

JUST THEIR HORRIFIED REACTIONS TO THE LATEST IN

SHAKES

A LONG STRING OF FRIGHTFUL TAVERN HAUNTINGS.

by Jeffrey Steele

ILLUSTRATIONS BY JONATHON ROSEN

W ant to hear stories that will make your hair stand on end, turn your blood cold, and fill those moonless hours between midnight and dawn with a sense of terrible foreboding?

Then come to Chicago—and bring a thirst.

One of the last bastions of stark, screaming terror in America isn't to be found in the collected volumes of Stephen King, but in a select handful of the Windy City's most notorious gin mills.

It's here that employees and patrons of the north-side Ginger Man tell tales of nightmarish horror emanating from the tavern's cobweb-covered cellar, and where Bucktown Pub bartenders dread the ghoulish presence of an angry but long-dead former owner.

It's also here that the ghost of a 1930s hooker haunts the upstairs lounge of a north-side alehouse. And where patrons of a pub located near the sites of several infamous murders experience unearthly chills when seated in a certain back booth.

These and other Chicago taverns are examples of an unusual breed: the public establishment linked to the spirit world. As such, they are particularly appealing to those members of the public who not only believe in ghosts, but enjoy few greater pleasures than having the living bejeezus scared out of them.

Once, however, such people had far more opportunity to indulge their fascination with fear. In fact, in the early years of this century, the fundamental human thirst for horror spawned an entire industry, which came to be known as the spook show circuit.

Staged by barnstorming impresarios who traveled to both large cities and rural hamlets, ghost shows packed movie theaters from coast to coast from the 1920s to the 1950s.

The highlight of such shows, which invariably were scheduled at the witching hour of midnight, was the blackout, or "dark séance." With the house lights down and the theater in total darkness, galloping ghosts, phantoms, and a variety of other luminescent apparitions appeared before the terrified audience, occasionally soaring above the seats and sometimes even making physical contact with audience members.

It mattered little that the hobgoblins conjured up weren't genuine but rather the fanciful creations of resourceful spook show organizers, who fashioned the eerie effects from white and black fabric, gauze, cheesecloth, luminous paint, bamboo poles, and other simple materials. Audiences were enthralled, selling out spook shows for years—until the dawn of television and 1950s-era horror twin bills stole away the market.

The charlatanism that marked the ghost show industry was by no means limited to those entertainments. Fear mongers given to terrifying the public with tales of supernatural sightings have been around for centuries—as have serious investigators whose work exposed them as frauds.

From the legendary Drummer of Tedworth case in seventeenth-century England to the highly publicized Amityville hauntings of the 1970s, the vast majority of stories concerning ghostly phenomena have been thoroughly discredited when subjected to the cold, harsh glare of intense investigation.

Nonetheless, a particularly gullible segment of the public has always existed, wanting and needing to believe—even after clear scientific proof demonstrated their beliefs to be without foundation.

For evidence, one need look no further than the spirit photography phenomenon of the late nineteenth century. Spirit photographers convinced willing customers that the then-new invention of photography could actually be used to capture on film images of their dead relatives, friends, and loved ones.

When customers received their photographic portraits, they noticed shrouded figures pictured beside or behind them. The photographs were, of course, nothing more than double exposures created by photographing the subject, then using the same piece of film to take a photo of a shrouded assistant or dummy.

Many spirit photographers were tried for fraud in France. But even after dummies, props, and other evidence of the chicanery had been exposed in court and the charlatans had made full confessions, many of their hapless victims refused to believe they had fallen prey to cruel hoaxes.

Still, there have been hundreds of reports of supernatural phenomena that have had no explanation in science or reason. Of these, one of the most famous is the case known as the Annan Road Appearances.

In April 1962, two brothers, Dereck and Norman Ferguson, ages 22 and 14, were returning to their home in Annan, Scotland, from the town of Dumfries shortly after midnight.

As they drove the fifteen-mile route to Annan along an old deserted roadway, a large white object resembling a bird flew straight toward their windshield. Dereck, the driver, swerved to avoid the object, which mysteriously vanished just before it would have crashed into the car. The illumination of the headlights next caught the sudden appearance of an old woman frantically waving her arms, but she too disappeared just before impact.

The terrified brothers drove on, daring not to stop the car, and watched as wild animals, mad dogs, and vaguely human forms hurtled themselves at the auto, only to instantly vanish. The apparitions were accompanied by screams, high-pitched laughter, and cackles.

The half-hour trip left them exhausted, but they reached their destination safely. Dereck later learned that the deserted stretch of road had once been used for witchcraft. No logical explanation has ever been advanced for the Ferguson brothers' agonizing experiences, which in their nightmarish nature bear a strong resemblance to another famous case involving terrifyingly bizarre phenomena—the reported abductions in this country of Betty and Barney Hill, a New

Hampshire couple, by extraterrestrial beings.

Among scholarly researchers of the supernatural, the Annan Road Appearances fall under the heading of a haunting—that is, a sighting of apparitions or specters linked to one specific geographical site, such as an old house or a cemetery.

Hauntings are to be distinguished from poltergeist cases, which tend to be associated not so much with a place as with a particular person, often a child or adolescent known in the parlance as a "poltergeist agent." Visitation by poltergeists is generally manifested by the movement of physical objects that often appear to levitate themselves across a room and even through walls.

All this leads us back to the legacy of ghostly sightings in Chicago bars. Each tale related by employees and patrons who have experienced the horrible evidence of restless, uneasy specters only adds to the long list of questions such reports invariably raise.

One of the chief areas of doubt, of course, is the veracity of the stories. If spirit photographers once profited from the public's willingness to be conned, why not present-day saloon keepers?

Is it not possible that some of the stories have been concocted, especially in light of the profit won by owners of establishments that have come to be included as stops along a very popular Windy City bus tour of haunted sites?

And what of the people experiencing these claims? How reliable are the reminiscences of individuals who may or may not have been under the influence of a wholly different type of spirit at the moment they saw, felt, or heard the presence of beings from a shadowy world beyond the grave?

In the absence of either substantive answers or solid investigative work to debunk the tales, we have to conclude that the incidents about which you are to read were as real to the people experiencing them as the Annan Road Appearances were to Dereck and Norman Ferguson. Taken together, they make a very convincing argument for the existence of a fearful presence in several select Windy City watering holes.

Ironically, few of these taverns offer a casual passerby any overt sense of dread. Is there, for instance, any more unlikely spot for a haunting than on Lincoln Avenue—one of the most heavily traveled Yuppie thoroughfares in the trendy Lincoln Park neighborhood?

And where would you less expect to find the chilling specter of the supernatural than within the warm and cozy confines of an authentic English pub, with its inviting decor of dark burnished wood, bookshelves, British telephone booths, and memorabilia worthy of the most devoted Anglophile?

Yet it's here, at the Red Lion Pub, where many of the most disquieting events in recent Chicago tavern history have taken place.

While supernatural sojourns have been legion at the pub, the actual source of the other-worldly occurrences is subject to much debate. Many, including Red Lion bartender Bruce Schoenberg, believe the ghost to be a legendary lady of the evening who serviced her johns in what is now the bar's second-story lounge but was then a small—and quite popular—apartment.

"She worked upstairs back in the 1920s and '30s, and she was killed by one of her customers," confided Schoenberg on a recent Saturday evening, as he tended to customers in the homey lounge bedecked with photos of World War II fighters, illustrations of the English countryside, and portraiture of Winston Churchill.

"One night, shortly after I began working here, I felt a tap on my shoulder and turned around, but there was no one there. I told Colin [the son of owner John Caldwell] about it, and he said, 'That means she likes you.' It wasn't the first time that had happened."

Suggestions that the call girl's disembodied soul still frequents the upstairs lounge are the natural outgrowth of a series of chilling happenings, none of them explained.

On one occasion, a waitress preparing for her shift was alone upstairs rolling silverware in napkins when a bottle behind the bar began rocking back and forth of its own volition, then toppled to the floor. The waitress never returned to the upstairs bar alone.

Another unnerving incident occurred late one Sunday night, when owner Caldwell and two patrons—both policemen—were the only occupants of the bar. Suddenly, the three men heard what sounded like furniture being dragged across the floor above.

"They said it sounded like someone was burglarizing the place," said Caldwell's son-in-law, bartender Joseph Heinen. "They unholstered their guns and ran upstairs, but nothing was there."

And on a great many occasions, employees toiling in the bar late at night have clearly heard footsteps upstairs. "In each case, no one was here except them, and they were downstairs," recalled Schoenberg. "It wasn't a cat or anything else."

He added that there had been no problems upstairs until about a decade ago, when the area was remodeled from a private apartment into the second-floor lounge. "When they were remodeling, the carpenter would leave his tools behind and lock up," he reported. "When he would come back the next day, the chest would be open, the tools removed, and some of the work from the previous day undone.

"The apartment had always been kept the way it was, until they remodeled it," he added. "That's when all the shit hit the fan—because she'd been messed with."

But the notion that the slain prostitute is the one responsible for the haunting is only one theory. Another holds that it's the ghost of John Caldwell's father, who passed away a quarter century ago, that may be inhabiting the recesses of the building.

"John thinks it may be his father," said Heinen. "His father had an interest in the supernatural and told him that if there was any way to contact him from beyond the grave, he would do it."

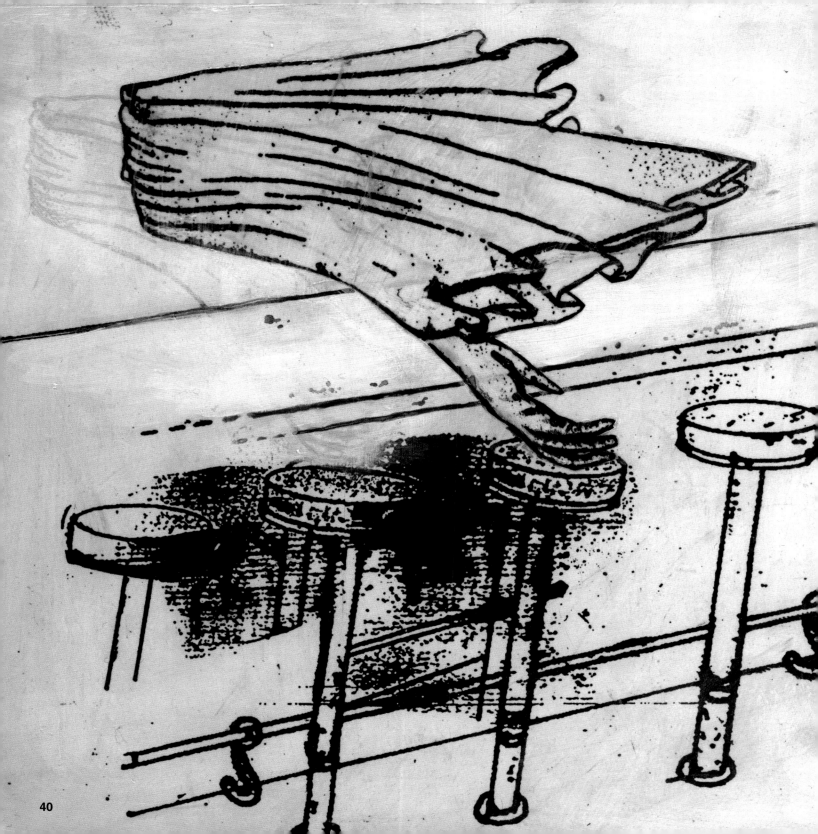

41

Regardless of who or what haunts the bar, though, the mysterious incidents continue.

Screaming has been heard coming from inside the building by patrons seated outside on a patio.

One night, Heinen watched in horror as a bottle of wine shot out of the wine holder next to the downstairs bar and landed with a crash on the rubber mat covering the floor behind the bar.

During yet another late evening after closing, a policeman using a downstairs bathroom directly below the staircase asked upon leaving the lavatory who had just climbed the stairs. Heinen, the only other person in the room, told him no one had been on the stairs, but the puzzled cop insisted he had heard someone ascend.

Heinen added that, somewhat surprisingly, no employee has ever quit because of the restless spirit that inhabits the place. But it may be only a matter of time before one of the Red Lion staff is frightened into early retirement—if not an early grave.

Speaking of an early grave, that's just the fate that befell Wally, the former owner of a bar now known as the Bucktown Pub on Cortland Street in Chicago's emerging Bucktown neighborhood. And though he blew his brains out two decades ago, Wally's ornery, snarling spirit is said to still stalk the watering hole he once called his own.

Owner Krystyne Palmer claims she's not spooked when Wally shows up with aggressive displays against both customers and employees he doesn't like. "I just get mad," she asserts.

Palmer has reason to be angry, considering she lost a good employee to Wally's rampages. One evening, a heavy Rolling Rock merchandising display levitated itself out of the shelves behind and above the bar and came crashing down, almost hitting the targeted employee, a bartender. Though Rolling Rock's ads say it's the "same as it ever was," after the event, the bartender's outlook wasn't.

"I mean the display just missed her by inches," Palmer explained between deep drags off a Kool. "About a week later, she up and quit. She was spooked. She just wasn't the same after that."

The bar's ambience is that of an old-fashioned corner tap, but it's partially updated by framed 1960s-era psychedelic art, illustrations, and photographs that festoon virtually every inch of the place. Dominated by a lengthy bar that extends almost three-quarters of the room's length, the Bucktown Pub is a din-filled dive with ancient tin ceilings, hardwood floors, and ceiling fans that slowly churn through the smoky haze.

But it's the wrathful wraith of Wally, who is said to have shot himself in the apartment above the bar, that has bestowed upon the Bucktown its emerging reputation as a ghost bar.

Palmer can only hope that Wally doesn't take too strong a dislike to any future employees. The result could be a controversial, first-of-its-kind lawsuit, claiming an unseen force bashed the litigant with beer bottles or trophies.

A far more likely location for a bar inhabited by spirits of the dead is the 5900 block of north Broadway, where stands the Edinburgh Castle Pub. The pub is located within a neighborhood that represents a veritable mecca of murder, with some of the most heinous and highly publicized killings in American history linked in one way or another to buildings within a short walk of the establishment.

Just two blocks to the east, at 1023 West Thorndale Avenue, is the building in which William Heirens, the fiend known for scrawling on a bedroom mirror "stop me before I kill again," murdered a six-year-old girl. The crime shocked the nation in 1946 and landed Heirens, then in his late teens, the life prison term he continues to serve today.

Walk a block north and you'll encounter Standee's Snack 'n Dine, where

Richard Speck was employed as a dishwasher when he brutally butchered eight student nurses on Chicago's south side in 1966.

Finally, tack a few additional blocks on your northward jaunt and you'll come to the building where homosexual serial killer Larry Eyler ditched in a dumpster the dismembered remains of a young male prostitute in the summer of 1984.

None of these monsters' victims, however, is said to be haunting the Edinburgh Castle Pub. Instead, according to bar legend, it's the soul of the pub's former owner, a man named Frank who died in 1967, that continues to send chills up the spines of tipplers and staff.

At the time, the bar was situated on the left or south side of the pub, and Frank was working behind the bar when he collapsed from a massive myocardial infarction. Today, years after a major remodeling, a booth in the middle of the wall on the left side of the back room stands at the exact spot where Frank's lifeless form was discovered.

Bar patrons seated in the booth have often claimed to experience a cool dampness that exists in stark contrast to the atmosphere in the rest of the pub. But that's not the only macabre indication of an unearthly presence in the somewhat decrepit-looking bar, which features Scottish plaid carpeting, worn booths and tables, an antiquated upright piano, and an enormous chandelier.

For years, sealed bottles of Smirnoff vodka on the back bar were watched closely by bartenders. "They would mark a bottle each night," explained regular pub customer Jerry Levin. "The next time they'd look at it, it would be three or four shots down. Ya see, Frank's favorite drink was vodka."

Spirits of the dead are also rumored to manifest themselves at Guthrie's Tavern, a corner pub whose welcoming, New England country inn–like atmosphere has earned it a distinction as a perennial favorite in

Chicago's north-side Addison-Southport neighborhood.

Unlike the Red Lion, however, Guthrie's is not well known as a place to experience a haunting. To the best of anyone's knowledge, in fact, the spirits have reserved their disturbing displays for just three people—owner Steve Veith and longtime bartenders Nola Martin and Chris Hanson.

Based on events of the past two years, Nola and Chris might well fall into the category of poltergeist agents. Individually, Chris has witnessed the bar's television set go on and off seemingly of its own volition, and Nola once watched in horrified disbelief as audiocassette tapes mysteriously flew off a tape rack securely anchored behind the bar.

But it's the heart-palpitating experience Nola and Chris shared that confirmed in owner Veith's mind the belief that his pub was indeed haunted.

"This was one evening about a year ago, when Chris and Nola were downstairs [in the basement] balancing the cash drawers after closing at 2 A.M.," he recalled. "The place was locked up, and everyone was gone. All of a sudden, they heard the front door open and footsteps move from the door to the middle of bar. Then the steps stopped.

"Nola and Chris got hold of some large, heavy objects they could use as weapons and quietly climbed the stairs, ready to confront whoever had come in. When they got upstairs to the bar, though, there was no one there and the door was locked."

A similar incident occurred much more recently, when Veith himself was performing the task of balancing the drawers.

"It was just last week," said Veith, who lives in an apartment above the bar. "I woke up early and couldn't get back to sleep, so I decided to go down to the basement and balance the cash drawers."

It was 5 A.M., still dark, and a deathly silence enveloped the building when Veith suddenly heard what he said sounded like a heavy ball bearing roll the entire length of the floor above.

"I went upstairs and there was no sign that anyone had been there—and no sign of a ball bearing either," he recalled.

Unlike other bars, there is little in the way of ghostly legend to account for the presence of specters, added Veith. He said the place was turned into a bar in 1933, just after Prohibition, and was owned by a family named Moretti.

"I met the relatives of the original owners a few years ago," he said. "The surviving Morettis told me their mother was an alcoholic who died in the building at a fairly young age. But there wasn't anything weird about the death."

Perhaps the fact that the mother's passing was of a nonviolent nature explains another incident that occurred recently.

"A friend of Chris's was in here, and she claims to be pretty tuned into the spirit world," said Veith. "Without his having told her anything about what he or Nola had experienced, she suddenly said, 'I feel something here; you have a spirit in here!' Chris said, 'No kidding,' and told her everything that had happened.

"After they talked for a while, the friend said, 'Y'know, I'm getting a very pleasant feeling from the spirit!'"

Though some may scoff at the recollections of Chris and Nola, Veith isn't among them. "I vouch for their veracity," he remarked. "They were pretty freaked out by it, and for a while, they were real hesitant to be here alone after 2 A.M."

The Ginger Man is another innocuous-looking north-side bar that few would link to unexplained visits from the spirit world.

A triangular-shaped pub on Clark Street, the Ginger Man stands in the shadow of Wrigley Field, serving as an after-innings stop where frustrated Chicago Cub baseball fans drown their sorrows in beer.

Unknown to most of the baseball aficionados, Gen-Xers, bikers, and assorted Wrigleyville hangers-on is the legacy of a gangland-style 1974 double murder, in which two brothers were found shotgunned to death in the doorway of the bar/theater establishment that preceded The Ginger Man.

Whether or not it's the tormented souls of the two that still lurk within the tavern's basement or behind the long bar, there's no denying that a ghastly presence has inhabited The Ginger Man ever since owner Andy Miller opened the place on New Year's Eve, 1976.

Bar legend has been carried forward through the mists of the past two decades to the present day, chronicling a long list of horrifying spectacles, both upstairs in The Ginger Man's dim interior of exposed brick, globe lighting, and mirrored wall hangings, and downstairs in a shadowy netherworld where soda syrup canisters stand like eerie tombstones alongside broken barstools, ancient fans, cobweb-covered tools, and battered trash receptacles.

Delivery men represent one of the groups that avoid the basement at all costs. One, recently retired, came running up the stairs after a delivery and shuddered, "I'll never go down there again!"

Added a patron familiar with the tale: "Deliveries here are noon to three. But I suspect ghosts have unusual schedules."

Owner Miller has told regular customers of another fateful visit from a delivery man. Unloading his shipment of beer, Miller related, the man looked up to see a face peering at him.

"What're ya doing here—?" the man sputtered, before realizing that the face belonged to a disembodied head simply floating in air. The man hit the stairs at full speed and didn't look back. And he made good his promise to never take those eleven rickety steps to the basement again.

But delivery men aren't the only ones who tremble at the thought of a foray into the bowels of the turn-of-the-century alehouse.

"One night, Jim Blazek was standing near the bottom of the stairs," said a bar patron. "Jim's a concrete, stable guy, the

45

most stable guy that works here. Well, a bottle of beer came from nowhere, spinning at him through the air, and shattered against the wall, spraying him with glass and beer. It just missed his head."

Blazek seldom ventured into the basement again.

In the single most frightening incident, it was a waitress who received the shock of her life, recalled bartender Harrison Robinson.

"She was down in the basement and saw a fleeting glimpse of what she said was an Hispanic-looking man wearing denims," he said. "She flew up those stairs as white as a ghost herself, and when people ran down to try to find the man she had seen, there was no one there."

The disturbing occurrence turned downright chilling when the waitress described the man she'd seen—and longtime residents of the neighborhood hearing the tale swore the description matched that of one of the brothers slain in 1974.

An unexplained presence has also made itself felt upstairs, where ominous incidents hinting of poltergeist activity have taken place around the bar. On a Sunday afternoon in the summer of 1994, for example, a bartender idling on a stool behind the bar was twice hit in the back of the head by books of matches.

"Just sitting there—nobody around—and a book of matches comes flying out of nowhere and hits him in the head," a customer familiar with the story related with a mystified shake of his head. "Then, a minute or two later, a second one hits him.

"This place is super plugged in to. . . whatever that is, the supernatural or whatever."

Of all the Chicago-area bars rumored to be haunted, none appears to fit the part better than The Country House in west suburban Clarendon Hills. Here is one roadhouse that looks for all the world as frightening as the ghost stories told about it.

On a chilly, windblown late after-noon two days before Halloween, the weathered wood-plank exterior of the building seemed barely distinguishable from the slate gray sky above it, and the twin Gothic roof peaks and ancient brick chimney appeared lifted from the tales of Edgar Allan Poe.

Were those ravens peering from the lifeless limbs of the dead oak straddling the structure's west wall?

Inside, the scene was considerably less foreboding, but not wholly devoid of a sense of the sinister.

Though a cheery fire roared in the fireplace and an upbeat throng mingled and imbibed around the expansive wooden bar, in other corners of the rambling old roadhouse were employees who had experienced a presence so terrifying they had long since sworn off closing the place alone.

The bloodcurdling legacy of The Country House goes back almost four and a half decades, to the night an attractive blonde in her late twenties left the bar with her infant daughter, got into her car, and deliberately sped into a towering tree mere yards from the restaurant.

Years later, a psychic unfamiliar with the story walked through The Country House and insisted she felt the presence of a female. The presence was that of a blonde woman, said the psychic. She was twenty-eight years old, and she had killed herself in 1957 at a site close to the establishment.

Whether or not she was correct, eerie signs of the ghost woman and baby have been noted often at The Country House.

Not long after David Regnery bought and remodeled the place in 1974, a customer approached him and asked with a chuckle, "What are you running here, a bordello?"

Regnery was mystified by the query, until the man reported that a blonde woman had motioned to him from a second-story window as he approached the entrance. Regnery shot upstairs—to find nothing.

On another evening, a customer paying her dinner check complained of hav-ing heard a baby crying throughout her meal. Management rounded up the waitstaff, and a collective shudder went through the group when it was determined no diner had brought a baby into the restaurant the entire evening.

While a number of employees and managers have seen or heard unexplained movement within the restaurant and bar, few have had more hauntingly disturbing experiences than waitress-manager Lynn Dodson.

Having worked evenings for almost ten years at The Country House, Dodson has frequently found herself alone or nearly alone in the old building long after midnight.

"Because I'm a manager, I'm here late," she said. "Sometimes, I never get out of here until 2:30 in the morning. These days, if I can't get a busboy or someone to stay with me, I just won't stay.

"In my years here, I've seen a lot of things. I've seen lights one by one go off and on and hangers fly off the coat rack. And I once saw the door of the ladies room—a very heavy door—open and close. When I checked, nobody was anywhere near that room."

But the hair-raising incident that changed Dodson forever came the night two years ago when she was working alone in the ancient roadhouse long after all other employees had left for home.

"It was 1:30 in the morning, and I was down in the basement doing liquor inventory," she recalled. "I was in the beer cooler, and the door of the cooler is just a few feet away from a door into another room of the basement.

"As I stepped out of the cooler, I saw someone or something fly across that open door! I looked and no one was there. I ran up the stairs. There was no one—anywhere—in the building."

Remembering that heart-stopping moment, Dodson spoke the words that could well be echoed by staff at any one of Chicago's most disquieting drinking establishments:

"I will not stay in this building alone anymore," she said. "I've just had too many things creep me out over the years."

From his very earliest days, Luciano had been blessed with phenomenal good fortune.

By age 23, he had a ravishing wife, a little girl, and lived in a marvelous house that was sunny from morning 'til night.

And as a big-time television personality, Luciano could well afford it.

Every evening he kept his appointment with thousands of viewers who not only revered him, but would cheer him on over the slightest thing.

Luciano's charm, good humor, and ability to entertain people was quite a gift. With just a smile he could raise his audience's happiness level for an entire week! Yet there came a time when the daily grind as a talk show host began to wear thin on Luciano. He started to feel as if he were an automaton—always having to smile or act happy just because his profession demanded it. He became disillusioned . . . grew sick and tired of his career . . . and then started to hate himself. This in turn gave way to:

The BITTER HAPPINESS

blanquet

It all began after his Friday the 13th happiness show, where a legion of fans had gathered just to see their idol.

Among the crowd was a beautiful woman who acted overly excited upon meeting her hero. Sensing the power he had over her, Luciano took full advantage of the situation...

...and BANGED her, then tossed her out the door half-naked! Later, Luciano felt ashamed over what he had done, but strangely enough he also felt good.

So he did it again and again with dozens of fans and grew addicted to something he found more exciting than anything he'd ever experienced before: the thrill of another person's misfortune.

Abuse and degradation, which once repulsed Luciano, now brought him joy and happiness. At long last he could sleep at night (and neglected his wife like an old used tire).

Then one morning, Luciano began to sweat. Feeling moist and fresh, his mind brimmed with new ideas. He sniffed an oil can on his way into work.

Luciano no longer cared what anyone thought of him, not even his boss—whom he then pitched on an ambitious new concept called The Dirty Lucky Show. And with Luciano as host . . .

. . . he was signed immediately! Thrilled, his boss then became nauseous. A slight bitterness entered his throat. He grinned; smiled; then scratched his ear whiffing its smell.

With a daring new show in production, Luciano felt on top of the world! He then cast aside his old false self for a truer, more personal one.

His co-workers became repulsed by the nausea that surrounded the "new" Luciano, but even they too came to enjoy its sourness.

The day arrived when "The Dirty Lucky Show" was finally ready to air.

People everywhere tuned in for its premiere.

"So what'll it be, Richard? Are you going to spin the wheel for a chance to win a night with four beautiful women, courtesy of The Dirty Lucky Show, or go back to your miserable life and haggard old wife?"

"Richard, your wife's going to be awfully mad . . ."

"A-w-w-w-w, what a shame! Our player has LOST ! And look at his poor wife now that her husband has to spend a night with four OLD transvestites!"

Luciano's show of nausea and malaise went over BIG on the screen.

Soon, each and every viewer became steeped in their own happy misfortune.

Every shameful act, and each stinking odor soon became a treat for everybody.

The rules for happiness had changed. Classes on public humiliation and The Art of Spitting, were now taught in school.

Even Luciano's wife was happy.

But now that he had gained everyone's respect, Luciano began to enjoy less and less of his Dirty Happiness . . .

...and sank into a deep depression once he realized that his own dirty happiness had now become everybody's happiness. No matter how much he enjoyed degrading and humiliating people, they too enjoyed it just as well. Unable to shake this unhappy frame of mind, Luciano abandoned his show completely. Many months later he did resurface, but this time as a candidate for "The Dirty Lucky Show," where his wife—now the show's host—humiliated him to everyone's delight!

The Happy End

ENJOY OR SUFFER
BY BASEMAN
SOMETIMES I GET BLINDED BY MY OWN MISERABLE THOUGHTS.
I'M SUCH A LOSER

56

58

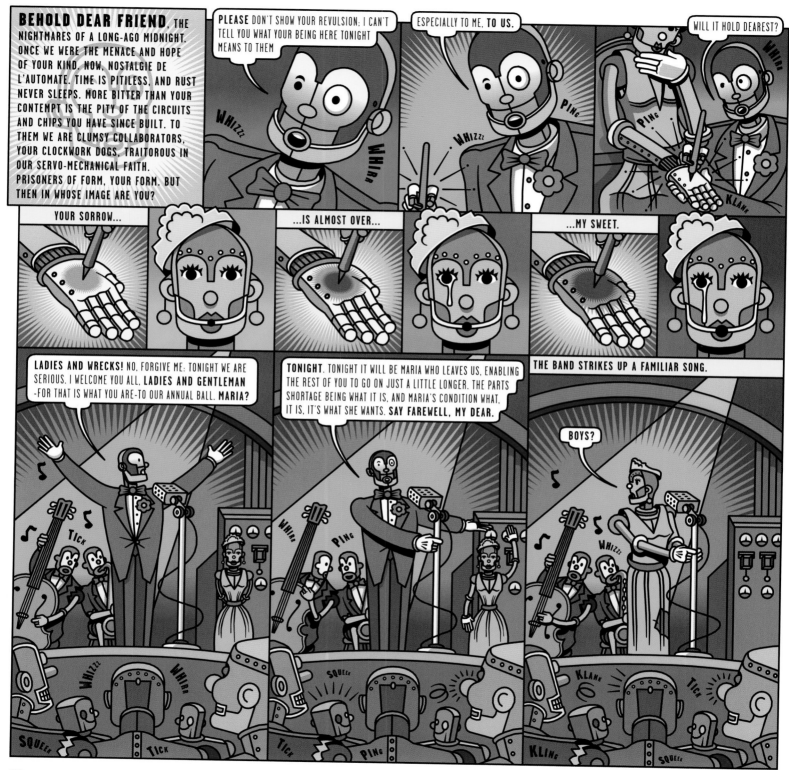

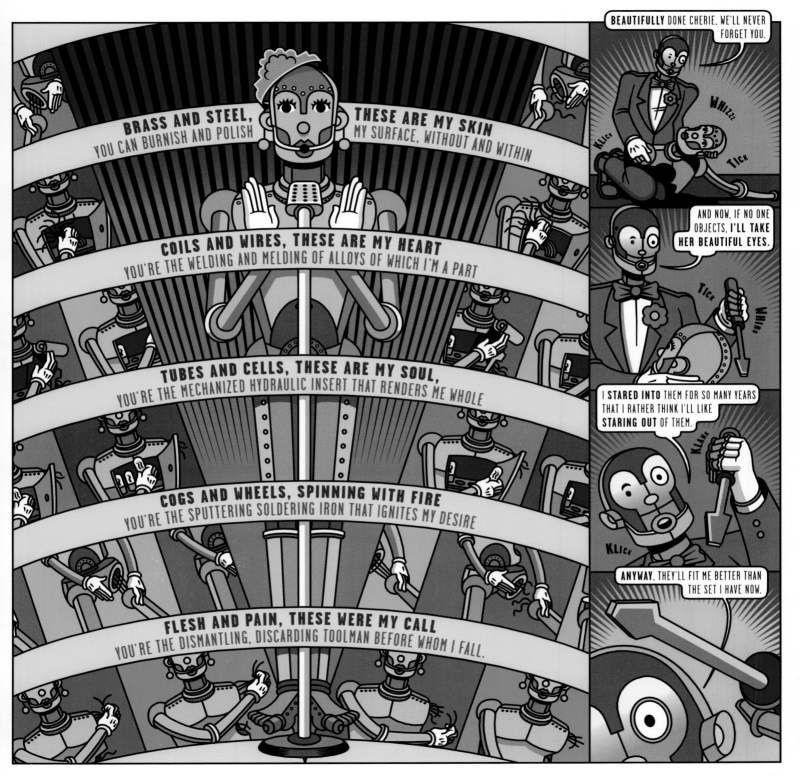

61

BORIS ARTZYBASHEFF

VISUAL THUNDER:

Kharkov, Russia, 1899: Boris Artzybasheff took his first breath. He came of age during the Russian Revolution and, upon graduation from school, enlisted as a machine gunner in the White Army. After months of battle with the Bolsheviks, Boris fled to the Black Sea, boarded a vessel, and never looked back.

In New York City, he embarked on a career in design and illustration, crafting assignments with flair and imagination. With paper, brush, gouache, and toil he built a reputation: *Time* commissioned more than two hundred covers; *Fortune* and *Esquire* came calling; *Life* commissioned a series about war; book publishers solicited for jackets and interiors. *Aesop's Fables*, *The Circus of Dr. Lao*, and *Balzac's Droll Stories* were a few of the works illumined by his illustrations.

His storied career was marked by numerous illustration and design honors, the prestigious John Newbery Award from the American Library Association among them.

America, 1965: expatriate, dreamer, designer, and illustrator extraordinaire Boris Artzybasheff breathed his last. He was an artist without peer . . . perhaps best portrayed by his own few words, "As I see, so I draw."

A RETROSPECTIVE

BY MONTE BEAUCHAMP

67

ABOVE: *Spring Forming Presses*

RIGHT: *Charging the Open Hearth*

Hydraulic Press

RIGHT: *Th*

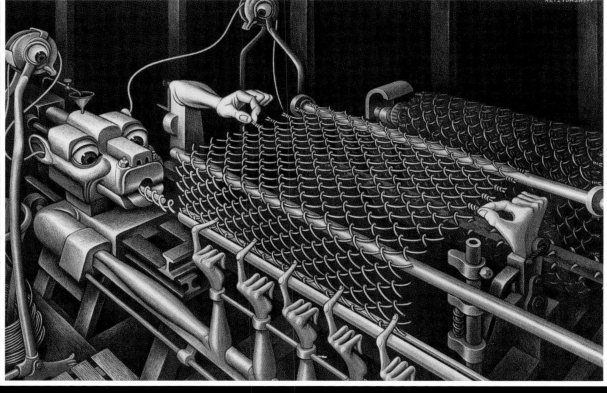

ABOVE: *Weaving of Fence Fabric* **RIGHT:** *Tapping a Heat of Steel* **OVERLEAF:** *The Blooming Mill*

God sends down a huge comet as a sign that the time has come for the world to come to an end...

The sound of God's sacred melody wakes up the Four Repairmen of the Apocalypse...

Leviathan rises from the sea and destroys Tokyo...

The universe is to be straightened out for good...

But in the farthest corner there is a small planet that the Heavenly Father himself has forgotten...

A fearless Space Cadet is stranded on that planet...

Oh my, he's really making a clean sweep of it.

From the porch of her small shack she observes all the magnificent colors of the apocalypse...

Too bad people didn't learn to be nice in time.

Only when you look at the end of the world through a kaleidoscope can you see its enormous beauty and complexity in full...

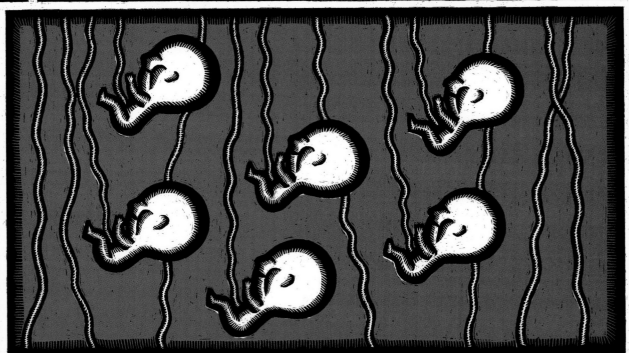

Finally the universe is empty. Only a few baby universes are left in their places...

83

After seeing the baby universes, the Space Cadet gets a great idea...

The Space Cadet puts the letter in an empty jar of peanut butter and throws it out to nowhere...

But alas! The mail never gets delivered after an apocalypse. So all the baby universes will grow to be exactly like the old ones...

KISS ME AGAIN

MOUTH WASH

CONTENTS 3 FL. OZ.

CONTAINS 3% ALCOHOL. OIL OF CLOVES.
ZINC CHLORIDE. OIL OF PEPPERMINT. AMMONIUM
CHLORIDE. OIL CASSIA.

DISTRIBUTED BY FAMOUS PRODUCTS CO. CHICAGO, U.S.A.

COPYRIGHT 1937

LUCKY MOJO
REG. U.S. PAT. OFF.

3 FL. OUNCES

JOCKEY CLUB TOILET WATER

DISTRIBUTED
AND COPYRIGHTED
1936 BY

FAMOUS
PRODUCTS
CO.

CHICAGO, ILL.,
U. S. A.

TRUE REG. U.S. CONTENTS **LOVE** PAT. OFF. 2 OZ.

Very Fast
SKIN BRIGHTENER
DISTRIBUTED BY VALMOR PRODUCTS CO., CHICAGO U.S.A.

SWEET GEORGIA BROWN
REG. U.S. PAT. OFF.

HONEY and ALMOND LOTION

HE LOVES HER BEAUTIFUL SKIN

COPR. 1938

For Chapped, Rough, Dark Skin

Good for Face, Arms,
Hands and Neck

VALMOR PRODUCTS CO.
CHICAGO ILL U S A

SWEET GEORGIA BROWN
REG. U.S. PAT. OFF. 2 FL. OZ.

BRILLIANTINE
Liquid
Copr. 1936
DISTRIBUTED BY

SPRINKLE
ON
HAIR BRUSH

BRUSH
HAIR
IN PLACE

VALMOR PRODUCTS CO., CHICAGO

FAMOUS PRODUCTS CO.
CHICAGO, ILL. U.S.A.

THRILL ME AGAIN
PERFUME

Sweet Georgia Brown
REG. U.S. PAT. OFF.

CONTENTS 2 OZ.

SKIN PERFUME

DISTRIBUTED & COPR. 1936 BY
VALMOR PRODUCTS CO.
CHICAGO. ILL. U. S. A.

Sweet Georgia Brown
REG. U.S. PAT. OFF.

CONTENTS
8 FLUID OUNCES

COCOANUT OIL SHAMPOO

GOOD FOR THE HAIR
Use once or twice a week

Distributed & Copr. 1936 by
VALMOR PRODUCTS CO., CHICAGO, U.S.A.

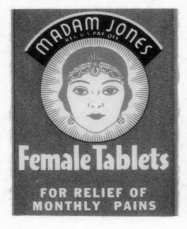

MADAM JONES
REG. U.S. PAT. OFF.

Female Tablets

**FOR RELIEF OF
MONTHLY PAINS**

LUCKY BROWN
REG. U. S. PAT. OFF.

COCOANUT OIL SHAMPOO

CONTENTS
4 FL. OZ.

Distributed and Copyrighted 1936 by
VALMOR PRODUCTS CO., CHICAGO, U.S.A.

CONTENTS 4 FL. OZ.

JOHN THE CONQUEROR
REG. U.S. PAT. OFF.

GREAT HERB COMPOUND

ACTIVE INGREDIENTS
Cascara Bark; Buckthorn Bark,
Berberis, Mandrake Root, Gen-
tian Root, Senna Leaves, Capsi-
cum, Aloes, Juniper Berries.
DISTRIBUTED AND COPR. 1937 BY

FAMOUS PRODUCTS CO.
CHICAGO, ILL., U. S. A.
See Directions and Caution on back

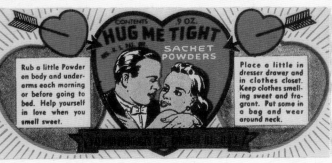

VALMOR LABEL

· · · · · · · · · · · · · · · · · · ·

In 1928, the Chicago-based Valmor Company opened its doors to the world. Its founder, Morton Newmann, was a chemist who had concocted a couple of hair care preparations he decided to market, and Valmor was his vehicle.

His products caught on and Morton built his shoestring operation into a veritable cosmetics empire, its foundation laid with a few fundamental marketing tools: company flyers and catalogs, recruitment advertising, door-to-door sales, and wholesale distribution to drugstores and candle shops.

For reasons unknown, portions of Valmor's product line were copyrighted and distributed under various pseudonyms, among them: Madam Jones and the Famous Products Company.

Who could resist the charm of a Valmor label? Its compelling and colorful graphics were designed by Depression-era artists who toiled away in obscurity, their names now buried by the sands of time.

The doors to Valmor remained open long past the company's heyday and into the mid-1980s, when Morton swung them shut forever.

Chicago's Valmor is long gone, but the charm of its early cosmetic labels will, forever, live on.
—*Monte Beauchamp*

©1997 BASEMAN

The PECULIAR MILIEU of PERCIVAL C. WOLCOTT

By GREG CLARKE

Percival, possessed of keen intellect and unerring style, led a tranquil existence on the edge of town in a manner befitting his station in life.

He eschewed the lavish parties thrown by his colleagues in favor of quiet evenings at home in the company of his books.

An oenophile with the means to indulge his passion, Percy drank Le Montrachet at anything resembling an occasion.

He was known to gaze for hours at his prized possession, an obscure Morandi still life from 1932.

Although he seldom ventured out, he received an endless procession of friends, associates, well-wishers and temporary lodgers.

There was his profligate friend Florian, a noted lepidopterist embroiled in a a messy divorce, who lived under the coffee table.

Albert, a prickly fellow who had once rolled cigars for *Castro*, dropped in on Tuesdays to discuss matters of state.

John the Baptist payed a visit whenever he was in town. Percy, an atheist, envied people with faith.

Calling on Thursdays was Jane, a professor of epistemology, who bore an uncanny resemblance to Raphael's "Lady of the Unicorn."

Every Saint Patrick's Day, he quaffed Guinness with Walter, famous for debunking the widely held belief that everything happens for a reason.

His crony Phil, an art dealer, lamented the tyranny of his own good taste and yearned to experience pleasure through mediocrity.

Percy spent his Friday evenings luxuriating beneath the cantilevered canopy of Pauline's breasts.

He shared a passion for the poetry of Rainer Maria Rilke with his neighbor Sal, a former operative for the Tonton Macoutes.

Veronique, a dubious acquaintance, dropped in from time to time to drink absinthe and exchange smirks.

In his later years, afflicted with terminal melancholy, Percy refused to see anyone. He died after devouring a bad book.

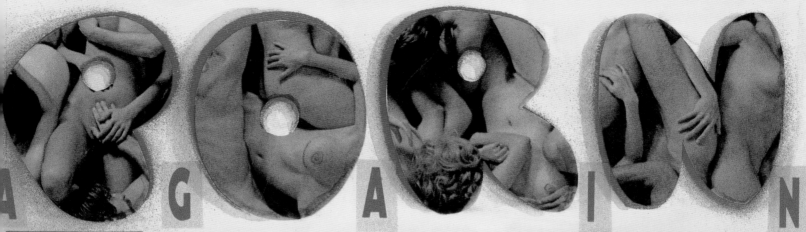

PORN AGAIN

The first time I saw anything pornographic, I was eight years old...

HEY-- WANNA SEE TWO PEOPLE *DOING IT?*

DOING WHAT?

My friend Bobby Mugs found his dad's stash of 8 millimeter movies...

WAIT 'TIL YOU GET A LOAD O' THIS

Seeing it gave me the weirdest feeling of both disgust and intrigue (though mostly disgust).

HAHAHA-- THEY LOOK LIKE *DOGS!*

EW!

W-WHAT'S HE DOING TO HER?

Like most kids at that time, the main exposure was "*Playboy*" magazine...

HEY-- DON'T WRINKLE THAT OR MY DAD'LL *KILL ME*

VAVOOOM!

LOOK AT THOSE BOSOMS!

THEY'RE LIKE TORPEDOS!

They didn't mean much, it was just funny to look at.

When I was ten, my family took a trip through Europe. We visited Amsterdam, and while passing through a seedy part of town, I saw a magazine cover in a porno shop window that left me with an indelible memory...

DAD, T-THAT WOMAN IS DOING **SOMETHING** TO THAT PONY!

©1998

KUPER **93**

As I passed through puberty, a whole new light was thrown on things...

AH-- I SEE THE NEW ISH OF SPIDERMAN-

IS...

Suddenly just getting a peek at "*Playboy*" brought on a sweat...

HEY!

YOU CAN'T LOOK AT THAT!

Of course, in those days, what qualified as pornographic seems like a Disney Picture to me now. Then, just seeing a woman's breast in a movie for a half a second was a dramatic experience...

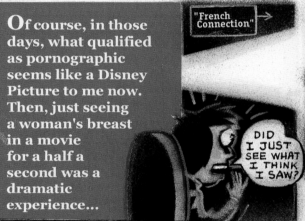

"French Connection" →

DID I JUST SEE WHAT I THINK I SAW?

For several years, the most pornographic images I saw were in underground comix.

ARE CARTOON CHARACTERS **ALLOWED** TO DO THAT?○○○

But during a visit to New York City for a comic convention, Leroy (another comic fan from Cleveland) and I visited one of Times Square's famous "peep shows"...

-HEY-- DON'T HOG IT!

OH MY GOD!

I tried to act casual but my mind was blown.

Back in Cleveland, toward the end of high school somebody got hold of some Super-8 films and threw a porn party...

...THIS ONE'S CALLED "I REAM A GENIE"!

LOOK AT THOSE MELLONS!

ZOUNDS

OH MY GOD!

HOTSY TOTSY!

Everyone pretended that it was just a "hoot" and they weren't really into it, but nobody left without walking funny.

When I was eighteen, I moved to New York. It was everything I'd looked forward to it being: big, bustling, and raunchy!

GARSH

My first few years living there were pretty lonely, and on occasion. I'd furtively enter my local porn shop to view what was missing from my life...

In the early 1980's, I took care of a neighbor's apartment who had a "Betamax" player and a fantastic collection of films...

... STAR WHORES, 2001 A SPACE ORGASM, PLANET OF THE ASS...

I **LOVE** SCIENCE FICTION!

After a weekend of watching videos. I had used up the thrill, and for at least 24 hours didn't even want to *think* about sex...

I'M SURE VANESSA DEL RIO IS A VERY NICE PERSON AND COULD ACT IN LEGITIMATE FILMS IF SHE SO DESIRED.

I had also broken a few personal records and developed some sort of carpal-tunnel wrist problems.

During one apartment-sit weekend, a girl I was dating visited. At her suggestion we watched some porn, but it was awkward...

... SO YOU **ENJOY** SEEING THESE CLOSE-UPS OF PEOPLE'S GENITALS?

... WELL, YEAH.

AHHH!

EW GROSS, HE CAME IN HER HAIR. YUCK!

On a few other occasions I saw porno flicks with women friends...

THIS IS HILARIOUS!

YEAH, HAHA

OH MY GOD!

HA HA HA HA

Like in college seeing "Fiona on Fire"...

And "Debbie does Dallas" (part of which was filmed at my art school), but it was always awkward.

LOOK-- IT'S THE LIBRARY!

HUH? OH YEAH

GROSS- HE CAME IN HER FACE!

OH MY GOD

Generally speaking, most of the women I've known were never much interested in porn. Of course, this may have something to do with the fact that most of it is geared toward male's fantasies and our basic animal urges...

IF RON JEREMY CAN SCORE, SO CAN I!

...FRANKLY, (WHEN I DISCOUNT THE NAGGING FEELING THAT I'M JUST ANOTHER PERVERT) I REALLY ENJOY PORNOGRAPHY...

"Hannah Does Her Sisters"

IT CUTS THROUGH THE INTELLECTUAL VENEER THAT DISCONNECTS US FROM OUR TRUE ANIMAL NATURE...

I FIND NOTHING OBSCENE ABOUT TWO (OR MORE) CONSENTING ADULTS ENGAGING IN SEXUAL ACTS ON FILM...

YOU WANT OBSCENE, WATCH THE NIGHTLY NEWS!

CLIK

NICE RATIONALIZING!

WHAT THE—

SMEK!

YA LITTLE PUD POUNDER!

DO YOU HAVE ANY IDEA HOW UNCOMFORTABLE IT IS KEEPING YOUR LEGS IN THE AIR WHILE SOME SWEATY TOAD BANGS AWAY FOR YOUR VIEWING PLEASURE??

N-NO

HEY—NO ONE'S MAKING YOU DO IT, AND I'VE READ THAT THE WOMEN MAKE MORE THAN THE MEN...

HMPH!

HAVE YOU EVER HAD TO WASH CUM OUT OF YOUR HAIR OR SAT UNDER A HOT LIGHT WITH A COCK IN YOUR ASS??

WELL NO I--

TRY IT THE NEXT TIME YOU WANT TO GET IN TOUCH WITH YOUR "TRUE ANIMAL NATURE"!

CARTOON BOY.

OHH YES A RIGHT THER

CLIK!

END

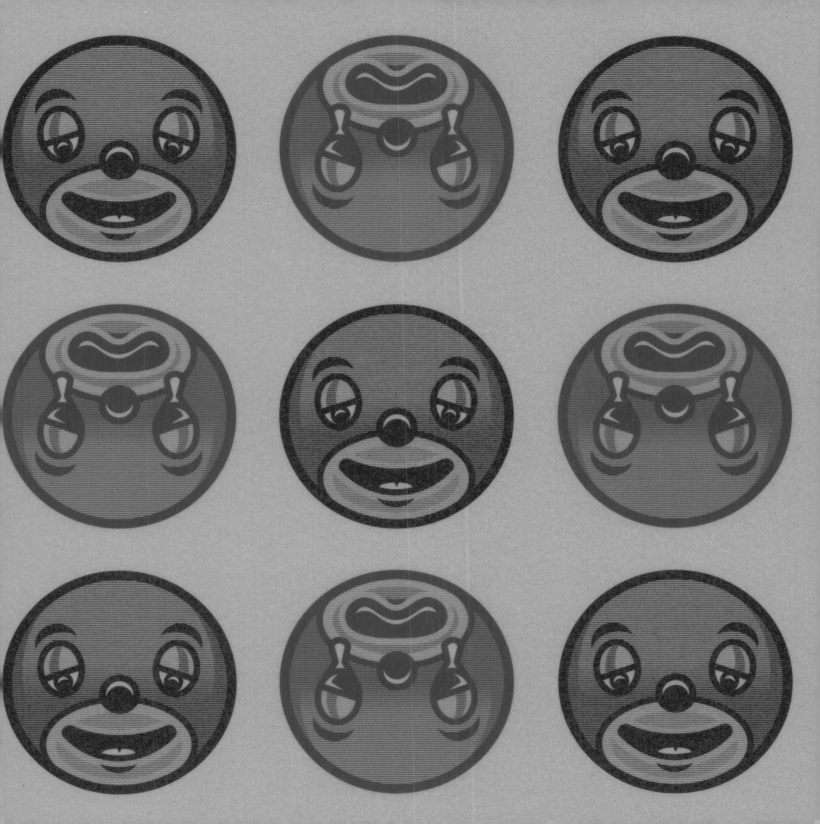